Come Away With Me

by

John A. Oliver
CB, PhD, RCDS, Hon.MRTPI

A warm invitation to share ...
in recalling seventy years of travel to unusual places abroad,
as well as the human interest behind them; backed by a
highly personal perspective from Ulster, and by still wider
experience with a recognized Centre of Excellence.

Published by

**MELROSE
BOOKS**

An Imprint of Melrose Press Limited
St Thomas Place, Ely
Cambridgeshire
CB7 4GG, UK
www.melrosebooks.com

FIRST EDITION

Cover designed by Sophie Fitzjohn

ISBN 1 905226 49 7

Printed and bound in Great Britain by:
CPI Bath, Lower Bristol Road,
Bath, BA2 3BL, UK

NOTE:

Publisher's Preface

These memoirs tell the story of many independant journeys made by John Oliver to places of special interest abroad, off the beaten track and beyond the normal tourist routes. He brings out again and again features of particular importance and deals with the many problems of language as they arise.

As his time-span stretches all the way from his school days in Ireland until his retirement seventy years later in Cumbria we find that there is an historical perspective that adds valuable depth to his vision of places and events in our rapidly changing times.

Not for him the Eiffel Tower or the Taj Mahal; he is more at home in Trois Rivières, or the village of Marathon or Gamla Uppsala; or even at the Krupp Armaments factory in Essen.

The author obviously enjoys bringing forward the humanity underlying many situations and he writes with a light touch and with more than a tinge of humour. He acknowledges the help given to him by his five much travelled sons.

As has often been said of his published short stories and essays it can also be said of these suprising memoirs that John Oliver entertains the reader at the time and yet leaves him or her with plenty to think about afterwards.

July 2006

With Supporting Photographs

1. Student card. 1936.
2. The parents. 1904.
3. John and his four sisters and two brothers. Belfast, 1984.
4. Quintin, Julian, Simon, Marcus, Myles. 2004.
5. The Magilligan Cottage, moved stone by stone to the Ulster Folk and Transport Museum, Cultra.
   With appreciation and thanks.
6. The Hezlett House, built 1691 at Castlerock, Coutny Londonderry.
   By courtesy of the National Trust. With appreciation and thanks.
7. We kept in touch.
8. Stella with John. London, 2002.
9. Mary Robinson, President of the Republic of Ireland with Quintin, one of her advisors.
10. Head stone, Nancy Oliver. Nancy was a valuable link in the American connection. Pennsylvania, USA, 1813-1901.

Contents

Appendix III On Magilligan

On Getting to know the Great
Essayist William Haslett

Part I

Come Away With Me

Introduction

When, in October 1932, I was moving up from
school to university (that is to say, from Royal Belfast
Academical Institution, popularly known as 'Inst', to
The Queen's University of Belfast) I had, like every
other student, to choose the main courses of study
I wished to undertake. The choice was not difficult
for I knew that my favourite schoolmaster (F. G.
Harriman, a strong and charismatic character) was
steering me in the direction of Modern Languages
(French and German). And so it turned out.

I have often wondered, since then, whether that
was indeed the best choice for me. I was certainly
interested in languages, in their history and
etymology and in their scope and strength in the
modern world. I realized, however, that I was not
an accomplished linguist and that I did not have
a particularly good ear for sounds and rhythms. I
was well aware that several of my contemporaries
were better equipped than I was. The three brothers
William, Sammy and David Moles in Belfast, as well
as that remarkable man J. J. Brown who could learn

the rudiments of a language in a week – to look no further – were better linguists that I was. Also and that R. J. Gregg of Larne had an exceedingly sharp ear for speech sounds; he used to amuse us with his ability to distinguish sounds used in one village from those in a neighbouring village – indeed from one Belfast street to the next. He later became Professor of Languages in British Columbia.

My choice of subsidiary subjects (Economics, Politics and Geography) tells its own story – two stories, in fact. If I had had to choose all my subjects a year or two later, I would probably have gone for PPE (Philosophy, Politics and Economics). While I had signed up for subsidiary Geography, I soon learned that Geography at Queen's meant, in practice, a foundation course in Geology. By a stern ruling of the university department no-one was allowed to take on a university course in Geography, in any land, and of any kind – physical, economic, racial, transport or whatever – without first learning what that region was made of. So our year was largely taken up with schist, gneiss, basalt, granite, oolitic limestone, alluvium and so on, leading on to scarp, dip, fault, oxbow-cut-off, drumlin, volcanic plug and so on. Botanists will applaud; even ornithologists will give a cheer.

But French and German had their own rewards. I quickly found the big wide world of foreign life and culture opening up for me – and the world of travel which has engrossed me all my life since then.

Here, for example, are four chances that happened to come my way in my student days. First, Inst sent me, at the age of eighteen, on a travelling scholarship to France; for the first three weeks to Paris under the tutelage of Madame Dauvé, widow of a French general and herself an educated and cultivated woman, who devoted herself to introducing me to the great churches, museums, galleries, opera, theatre, as well as those fascinating odd corners in old Paris. She even managed to include Père Lachaise graveyard. Then it was on to the seaside, to St Giles-Croix de Vie on the coast of La Vendée, where Madame Dubois had a summer place. Here there was company in plenty, with young French boys and girls coming and going, with tennis and bathing and lots of fun in the contemporary idiom of France at that time. One highlight was a visit from a travelling theatre speaking the most modern French 'argot'. Even as a boy I realized that my school had not only generously funded a fine scholarship but had most sensibly prepared the ground by carefully selecting, and consulting with, these two splendid women.

Then, at the age of twenty, I was lucky enough to benefit (along with my colleague Jack Crook) from an unusual and pioneering arrangement which Professor Gilbert Waterhouse had been able to make with the University of Königsberg to have us as registered students for one semester (six months running from April). The leap from Belfast to Königsberg was quite considerable, even though we could see some resemblances that might not otherwise be expected: each was the capital and main harbour of a province cut off from the mainland – Belfast by the sea, Königsberg by the hated Polish corridor from the German *Vaterland*. But the main attraction held good – the magnet of the University of Immanuel Kant, which was to influence us to a surprising extent in the key philosophical matter of epistemology – in plain words: existence, knowledge and reason.

Soon after we had settled in at Königsberg we were given a happy introduction to Frau Winternheim who occupied a fine house in the heart of the old town. Her husband was a dentist. Her father had been the Rev. Mr Patterson who had baptized me at May Street Church, Belfast, some twenty years earlier. Her ready welcome and hospitality helped to give us immediate insight into the professional and domestic life of East Prussia, for Frau Winternheim seemed to be as pleased to have us around as we were to come to her house for supper every now and again. We sensed a more mature stage which we were to come across often in Europe. British people who had emigrated became willing exiles or ex-patriots, but after a time they had begun to welcome any fresh connection with their homeland that came their way, as they consolidated a permanent position in their adopted country.

The following year came the totally surprising offer of a place at the Zimmern School of International Studies in Geneva, a small college run on democratic and liberal lines by Sir Alfred and Lady Zimmern, with staff on loan from various universities and about thirty students from some twenty countries in Europe and North America. The course was for three months and was, in a sense, residential as we all lived in approved lodgings grouped nearby. I had to 'room' with Maurice Oldfield who later became head of one of our secret intelligence services.

My biggest chance came immediately after graduation in the form of an advanced bursary that gave me a full academic year as a registered student at the University of Bonn at the height of Nazi power and influence in Germany. This was something really special, letting me see and experience many of the harder aspects of life in Europe.

Supporting that privileged position I lodged with a family in the centre of Bonn, a liberal stronghold that held out against most of the worst features of Nazi domination over academic life. The head of my family – Walter Breuer – had been incarcerated in a Nazi concentration camp and had lost his job as a resident magistrate. The outcome for me was that he was, frankly, out of work, and consequently free every day to spend time with me, often walking to the uni in the morning and greeting the attendants and staff with a cheery but defiant *Guten Morgen* instead of the obligatory *Heil Hitler.* Goodness knows how many other more serious indiscretions he committed in more sensitive quarters. Readers may be interested to learn that Stella and I are still in touch with the family all these seventy turbulent years later.

Perspective

Now, turning to our more personal ways of deriving benefit from foreign languages and foreign travel, I shall try to convey something of the way we have enjoyed travel in family and working life since then – that is, from 1937 up to the present time. I always think it right to start by placing such a varied experience in some sort of perspective.

Many young men of my generation travelled much further than I did and often in more difficult and dangerous situations. I was no dare-devil. Many had more time than I had, fewer deadlines to keep, more cash to spend. Those advantages are generally reflected in their more sophisticated style of writing. By contrast my style must seem simple, naïve, even jejune, albeit always in the dimension of seventy years.

To balance all that, I hope that readers may be able to discern a continuous thread of human interest seen against a background of history, geography and language – three of my abiding obsessions, however old-fashioned they may seem today. Having said all that, my approach is simply to relate the countless occasions when I – or my wife and I – made a planned visit to some famous city but deliberately went on from there to explore slowly some less well-known places, byways, off-the-beaten track, beyond the established routes of the tourist companies. This is not in any way meant to disparage organized tourism but just to suggest a streak of independence, even cussedness, in preferring to have my own way of doing things.

I have not attempted to place my different little trips in any sort of chronological order but rather in the order that I think best brings out the features and attitudes which I wish to stress. And I do not burden the text with dates, save occasionally to underline some bigger event or danger, such as Nazi interference in academic affairs in the 1930s or the tiresome blanket of restriction imposed on day-to-day life by the Communists before they had mastered the methods of tourism in the modern world and before they collapsed.

Help From Others

I was lucky to have much help from our sons who live and work in fascinating places. Without embarrassing them by drawing up a solemn league table of filial involvement, I shall confine myself to a tactful and restrained mention of the help they gave us in particular situations as they arose.

Readers who know me may wonder why I am not including Rhodesia and the beautiful countryside which I came to know so well, and spoke of so highly, while I was helping to supervise the famous General Election there in 1980. That was the election that made Rhodesia into Zimbabwe and made Zimbabwe independent. For one thing, I would have found it hard to line up the wide-open spaces of Rhodesia, far away in the southern hemisphere, alongside the tame little happenings, those local bus journeys and teashops in the settled milieu of European towns and villages. At a deeper level, and in the face of the tragic state to which Zimbabwe has been reduced, I cannot bring myself to give any breath of publicity or endorsement to the present regime, especially since it derived in a way from the very election that I had so closely monitored for its quality of being 'free and fair'. In a word, we had had a good election but a bad result. I say no more.

Still the human element keeps coming in. While working in Rhodesia I got much help from former pupils of Inst and Queen's working there. And I was proud to hear that in Presbyterian circles in Harare people were still talking appreciatively about my lifelong friend the Rev. Professor Jimmy Haire, on account of the scholarly work he did in translating the New Testament from Greek into New English. One of our great men.

Be assured overall that my story is truthful. None of it is invented. It all happened to me, or to Stella and me, supported by one or other of our sons.

Trois Rivières

It was not hard to pick out the various influences that combined to make the modern city of Montreal: the British, the French and the pervasive effect of modern capitalist America next-door. As I was admiring one day a fine seven-storey hotel there, I was bluntly told, 'We are just about to tear it down and put something twice as high in its place.' We made a point of visiting the two splendid universities, McGill and Notre Dame, symbolizing the inevitable clash of English and French cultures in many aspects of life there.

Feeling an urge to get out of the city and to see a bit of the great forest land of Quebec, we called at a bus depot in town and told the clerk that we wanted tickets to anywhere. From a list which he cited we chose Trois Rivières, simply because we liked the sound of that name and for no other reason.

Half an hour later we were travelling comfortably down by the St Lawrence River into dense forest terrain and soon reached the little town of Trois

Rivières. Here was a world apart. It was a town founded on the lumber industry, manufacturing newsprint for the newspapers of North America, exporting it through its own port, with its houses all made of wood (even the church clearly constructed of wood) and the people speaking French – even if it was the antiquated French of the original settlers in the seventeenth century rather than the modern French of today. As it happened, politics was in the air in connection with some outburst of the perennial agitation for freedom for the Province of Quebec from Canada – with the local hero and leader, Pierre Trudeau, taking a leading part in the local Liberal Party of which he was Leader and in the resistance to any breakaway, for he was at the same time Prime Minister of the Dominion of Canada – quite a difficult and dangerous position for any man to hold. But we admired and respected Trudeau and felt sure he would carry the day for common sense, as he did. I mention all this because loudspeakers on the streets of Trois Rivières were blaring out popular speeches – some carrying echoes of the famous outburst of General de Gaulle: *Vie le Quebec libre* – a most unsettling intervention, we thought.

Towards 4 p.m. children were coming out of school and our last image of the little town was of children boarding school buses in order to get to their homes still further off among the tiny villages and outposts of this wonderland – the Laurentian Shield, as it is called.

The Muggers Mugged

By happy chance one of our sons, Julian, had been lent by his employer to the Foreign Office and had been appointed Commercial Attaché at HM Embassy, Mexico City. Our stay with Clare and him was largely spent in and around the embassy, meeting his colleagues and associates and governed by severe security restrictions. Nevertheless, we saw enough to impress on us the go-ahead nature of the city and then the unfortunate contrast between the museums and galleries of world-class standard and the sight of many Mexicans literally sleeping in the gutters of that colourful capital, covered only by sheets of plastic.

Our wish to get away from the metropolis centred naturally on the urge to get as far as the Pacific Ocean. So, a short flight took us to Guadalajara and a second one to Puerto Vallerta on the Pacific coast and the opportunity to bathe in the Pacific. Otherwise the atmosphere and the detailed conditions in their reality on that coast were so American that they left little imprint on our minds. We came across American tourists everywhere, escaping from the cold weather in the USA that year. On return to Mexico City we were privileged to be invited to an embassy lunch at which Baroness Young, a Foreign Office Minister, was the main guest. However, for us, the highlight of the function was to hear the doyen of the Mexican commercial community publicly assure a large and influential audience that Julian Oliver was proving himself, by his work and achievements, to be the best Commercial Attaché Mexico had ever had, and asking to be quoted on that judgment.

Mexico City, crowded and turbulent, turned out to be the scene of an unusual occurrence – something that is seldom reported: the mugging of a bunch of muggers. Stella and I were assaulted on a city bus in broad daylight by an organized little gang of five young men who trailed us from some museums onto the bus. There they acted out their pre-arranged plan by showering us with a handful of small coins. Rising to defend Stella and myself, I merely made it easier for the leader to put his hand into my trouser pocket and remove my wallet. As I began to protest he put into force their drill of lobbing my wallet from one member of the gang to the other, carefully positioned at intervals along the bus. Once I saw that it had rested with their fifth man sitting in the middle of the back seat, in a commanding position, ignoring all risks and without any thought for grammar or syntax I accosted the chap, shouting repeatedly at him in Spanish, '*Donde porte-monnaie! Donde bolita!*' The character responded by fishing out my wallet from behind his back and meekly handing it to me, with all the valuables intact. The muggers had been mugged. Julian warned me afterwards that any one of those boys could well have had a knife. The significant feature of the episode from any public point of view is the fact that the one-man driver-conductor (who saw and heard all) took no notice and did nothing.

Marathon

One of our holidays in Athens, the one on which we had Quintin with us, illustrates particularly well the way in which we liked to combine serious study of the antiquities in the ancient city with the opposing attraction of the countryside and simpler pleasures.

With the memory of the gleaming mask of Agamemnon still in our minds, Quintin and I set off from a bus depot close to the Parthenon for a bus ride into the country – a matter of some twenty miles or so, we were told.

The destination turned out to be the old village of Marathon, totally unspoilt at that time, but with a good view out to sea from a local hillock. Joining some villagers at a simple wayside café and drinking lukewarm Nescafé with them, I played my winning card, the one that never fails to get us into happy carefree chat with men all over Europe: 'Of course you know that we are fellow compatriots in Belfast of Geordie Best.' Quintin, who was doing Greek at school at the time, took over the conversation and described in thrilling detail the great sea-battle of Salamis when the Greek fleet destroyed the Persians – and he was able to point out the very place in the sea where it all happened, helping to establish the greatness of Athens. Here Lord Byron had aptly summed up the situation for us, both geographical and historical, in his *Don Juan*, written around AD 1820: 'The mountains look on Marathon and Marathon looks on the sea'.

The twenty-six miles back to Athens that afternoon turned out to be rather dull, occasionally hilly, uninteresting – as others have found since then, some to their pain and some to their glory. My usual quest for the human interest behind great events was more fully rewarded than I had expected when Quintin reminded me that Pheidippides unfortunately suffered a heart attack after completing his pioneering Marathon run and died shortly afterwards.

Uppsala

Attending an international conference on housing in Scandinavia, I need hardly say, was an undiluted pleasure. Getting to see and hear the great architects and town planners of the day was, for me, an education; and being entertained by the inevitable conference wit was fun. His description this time of the popular lady organizer, 'sailing around her conference calmly, silently and unruffled like a swan, while pedalling away like hell underneath,' sticks in my mind

The extra interest this time was academic. When studying at Bonn on the Rhein some twenty-five years earlier I had had the good fortune to make the acquaintance and the friendship of two distinguished Irishmen, Michael Duignan and Seamus Carney, both of them Celtic scholars from University College, Dublin. They had in the meantime become leading scholars in Irish language and literature. Carney had been sent out by Dublin to help found a School of Irish as part of a general effort of the Dublin government to spread Irish through academic circles.

Actually his appointment, and that of his wife Maura, was not in Stockholm but in Uppsala, the true centre of scholarship in Sweden, we were told. This suited us well, as it let us get to know Uppsala further to the north. As it happened, they had teaching commitments in Gamla Uppsala (old Uppsala), still further north again, which once more suited us splendidly. The talk among the academics was all about publications, periodicals and promotions, to say nothing of plagiarism and piracy. We are still in touch with their son, Paul, in Dublin 4.

I greatly admired this whole effort at spreading the

Irish language – even though it was not my field – and I wished that the administration in Ulster could emulate that effort by selling abroad the specialized knowledge they had built up in other fields.

Oslo

Instead of going straight to the big city, I chose this time to travel by boat from Newcastle-upon-Tyne to Bergen on the west coast of Norway – and what a boat! It had been designed precisely for the job, and in those days we were apt to compare every ferryboat with our drab old Larne-Stranraer steamer. This ship had the luxury of beautiful, cheerful green carpet everywhere on deck, including the deck exposed to the elements.

Bergen combined the remnants of its mediaeval greatness as a shipping port with its present-day shipbuilding yards in a happy blend. And of course there was the home of the composer Edvard Grieg to visit, with its memorabilia of Peer Gynt.

My first shock in Norway was to find that the cost of living in 1977 was exceedingly high – some twice the level of that in Britain. I had thought that the arrival of much wealth from North Sea oil would have made everything cheaper, but apparently the gloomy science of economics does not work that way.

Then over bleak, empty mountainous territory

to Oslo, where our son Myles was studying Norse language and literature, taking a qualification first in the language itself (a more complex matter than might appear because of the dichotomy between regional and national versions) and second, in competence to teach Norse to others. (With all due respect to his professors, we found it hard to see where the demand for such a skill was likely to come from; but no matter.)

I need hardly stress the attractive aspect of their form of social democracy that struck me in Oslo, because every visitor has something of the same experience. For me it arose quite simply as Myles and I were walking together along a city-centre street when he suddenly pushed open a door, stepped inside and motioned me to follow him, saying quietly (and with no sense of occasion or formality), 'You are now in the Norse Parliament.'

On a Royal Farm

The peculiarity of Denmark which I would normally try to emphasize in a memoir such as this simply never struck me at the time: the place is so well-run; the people are so tolerant and reasonable; everything seems so settled, despite the awkward geography of managing a kingdom broken up into so many pieces of mainland and so many islands, so close to its neighbouring countries yet so separate and distinctive.

I shall content myself with recording just the two places that I liked most. One was the farm near Copenhagen occupied by the Danish Royal Family, that we felt we had to see as our boy Marcus had spent a useful working holiday there. Allindemagle, near Ringsted, Sjælland, was owned by the then Princess Margrethe, now Queen Margrethe II of Denmark. The farm manager, Gunnar Kristoffersen, and his wife Ethel ran a mixed farm, with a small herd of Danish Red dairy cows, Landrace pigs for bacon, and some cereals. The dairy herd was, unusually, kept inside during the summer, and fed freshly cut Lucerne every day in a bid to maximise grazing efficiency. The farmhouse, farm and buildings were immaculately maintained.

As with the Danish Royal Family generally, Princess Margrethe favoured an informal style and maintained a typical farmhouse on one side of the farmyard. On her frequent visits to the farm Princess Margrethe made a practice of always having a discussion with Gunnar on the current problems of managing the farm and with Ethel on the domestic arrangements. As parents we like to think that it was one small outcome of her visits that Marcus was served at table with a delicious substance they called 'black butter' as a novel complement to the vegetarian diet which he favoured all his life.

At the end of the summer work period Gunnar and

Ethel helped Marcus to arrange and book a return rail and ferry journey back to Belfast via Falster, Lolland, to Rostock, East Berlin (in the Democratic Republic of Germany), West Berlin (the Federal Republic of Germany), and so to Belfast.

Odense on the island of Fyn had to be seen for the sake of Hans Christian Andersen, the world-famous author of fables – 'The Ugly Duckling', 'The Snow Queen' and many others – a model for the presentation of such an unpretentious country house and its mementos. When I got back to my office in Stormont I passed on the word that every Borough Surveyor, or the like, should try hard to get a visit to Copenhagen in order to see good, simple, municipal order in force in many forms and at a level of cost that we could afford, unlike Stockholm where the level was well above the capacity of any normal community.

Enkalon

One of my duties for a time at Stormont had been to make sure that incoming new industries were supplied with all the infrastructure that they needed. One may scoff at the use here of that tired old portmanteau word, but it served us well at the time and embraced – just wait for it – water, dispersal of effluent, special dispersal of poisonous effluent, roads, bridges, electricity, gas, housing for workers, housing for managers, clinics, schools, technical classes for apprentices, and much else. The new companies differed greatly in their demands and Enkalon (the big Dutch artificial fibre concern) were amongst the most demanding. Nothing but the best. Thinking that I would be a slow learner and anxious to impress me, the company went out of their way to invite me to visit one of their existing plants in Groningen, a remote province of Holland away to the northeast and by no means their most promising area. And they insisted that my wife was included in the invitation.

We went. We were genuinely impressed – so much so that we began to suspect that this might be a showpiece dressed up to dazzle us and far beyond the normal standards of the country. Obviously in no position to make a weighty comparative study of industrial concerns in the Netherlands, as the Dutch people prefer to call their country, we decided to leave it to luck and to keep our eyes open.

Luck served us well. Deciding to call on our niece Jennifer on our way home, we made the necessary detour to the province of Brabant in the extreme southwest of the country. Jennifer, a North Country girl married to a most learned and accomplished Dutch lecturer, had hardly settled us into her house when she had to go and answer a knock at the door. Back in a moment she said to us, 'There is something here at the door which you ought to see.'

At the door stood a smart, gleaming white, walk-in van with shelves stacked with milk, buttermilk, cream, cheese, yoghurt and every brand of dairy product, all lightly chilled and forming a routine delivery of such things to households like Jennifer's. We were dazzled. The standard was of the highest: hygiene, variety, attractiveness and convenience combined. If Groningen could do it, Brabant could do it and Holland could do it – and we should be able to do it also.

Lourdes

If you had asked me in my earlier years what I thought of those pilgrimages to Lourdes by sick and crippled people in search of a cure for their ailments I would, to my shame, have dismissed the whole affair as a pathetic survival of rank superstition. Time it was all swept away. No place in the modern world.

When visiting Simon one time in the industrial city of Toulouse we noticed, from a rough sort of map in a shop window, that Lourdes lay less than an hour by rail from Toulouse. Arriving in the town of Lourdes we saw that we were lucky to have struck a day that had some special significance in connection with Saint Bernadette, the local girl on whose visions the whole edifice of the shrine is founded. The outcome was a particularly long procession of pilgrims and an atmosphere of total absorption and attention – with all the little shops open and offering their tawdry geegaws of popular Catholic culture, their trivial mementos, glass globes revealing 'The Manger' in a snow-storm, if you please.

Looking more closely, we could see that alongside the sick and the maimed in their wheelchairs and their pushcarts were necessarily their drivers, friends and supporters. Each little group carried aloft a banner: Barcelona, Andalusia, Macedonia, Scotland, Ireland, and so on and on. Gradually the truth was coming at us: the pilgrimage was based not only on the faith of the afflicted but equally on the love and care of an even greater number of supporters. It all mattered.

Then to the church where the sermon was being preached by no less a person than the Bishop himself. Here I was captivated by his use of well-prepared, classic French prose, skilfully balanced and elegantly delivered. Aware that I am prone to be influenced by eloquence of that kind and remembering my own appetite for clear, logical speech, I strove to make sure that 'form' was not obscuring 'substance', nor 'appearance' 'reality'. Far from it. The homily by the Bishop was deliberately concerned with the virtue of compassion, which he first analysed and then pronounced in a way, and with a weight, that affected me deeply. Faith and morals prevailed that day. Not given to sudden conversion, I nevertheless shifted the balance of my mind some considerable distance and that of my feelings as well.

Megève

The Chief Medical Officer of the Northern Ireland Ministry of Health (Dr James Boyd) received through medical professional channels in 1953 an invitation to nominate someone to take part in a conference in France on the general subject of the most suitable forms of organisation for a national health service. The requirements for taking part were familiarity with problems of structure, organisation and financing of any such concept, as well as ability to read and speak French fluently.

After taking soundings in medical quarters in Belfast, Dr Boyd found himself unable to nominate any suitable man or woman. As a last resort he fell back on me and begged me to help him out. I finally agreed. The venue was to be Megève, a ski resort in the Haute Savoie, near Annecy and not far from Mont Blanc, with good accommodation and services available off-season – in our case July. After preliminary talks with the organizers, it was agreed that I should kick off with a keynote address on the experience so far of the British National Health Service, while others would speak on the situation in their respective countries and their hopes for the future.

My assignment did not prove too difficult. For one thing I was at that time deeply involved in helping to set up our version of the NHS in Northern Ireland, with the advantage of being able to learn from the great experiment of Nye Bevin in Great Britain. I had been interested in the philosophical background to the whole idea, and I was giving evening classes on the subject under the Workers' Educational Association.

Another built-in advantage for me was the clear-cut, blue-water contrast between the basic British approach of one health service, free at the point of need, and the most widespread arrangement on the Continent of a multitude of services depending on insurance, contributions and subsequent reimbursement. A good conference ensued. And I assure my present British readers that I took every opportunity to warn against the inevitable rise in the cost of any free service and the even more probable escalation in demand from patients.

One of the by-products of such an international conference is the opportunity to get to know some leading personalities from other countries and to influence them in deciding to locate future meetings in Ulster. I was especially glad to find Professor Aujaleu of Toulouse ready to follow up these and other suggestions, for the French are not always the best or the happiest of travellers.

Any problems during the conference were lightly swept aside on the final evening at a splendid banquet when I was in a position to express (what I sensed other delegates had been privately thinking) the striking likeness of a rather too solemn clinician to that popular cartoon character of the time: Tartarin de Tarascon, the intrepid, daring, fearless Alpinist climbing Mont Blanc next door.

Ostia

A day's visit to the port of Rome (which is both ancient and modern) opened our eyes to much of the reality of the ancient world. Where we had thought that the Romans had led a static life apart from their military and colonizing adventures, we soon found that they had in fact been inveterate travellers – and in several different guises.

Foremost in their minds was the constant urge to consult the oracles wherever they might be, in order to take advice and instruction from the gods, who played an effective role in people's lives and in their decision-making in particular. And oracles seem to have lived in some remote and awkward places. Like the modern Germans, the Romans placed great faith in health cures and consequently travelled far to reach their favourite healing waters.

Then a walk around the harbour of Ostia convinced us that those famous straight-line 'Roman roads' that we all admire across Europe could not have been built and maintained without an immense use of manpower that had to come from somewhere. This applied even more to the Roman policy of going to the trouble of paving their roads. Add to that the many rest-houses that supported and fed the military troops, as well as the *cursus publicus* (a form of postal service) and the *mulomedici* (veterinary personnel), most of which would have started off here at Ostia.

Trade follows the flag. The export-import business with Britain, Gaul (divided into three parts, as Caesar tells us), Spain, Portugal, North Africa and the Middle East must have been considerable, and what more suitable and convenient trading point, storage place or commercial depot could there be than Ostia, a few miles from the great city on the one hand and on the other looking out onto the Mediterranean, 'the middle of the earth' as they knew it.

An intelligent people, proud of their military achievements and understandably inquisitive about the stories, legends and gossip that came their way from those outlying colonies, the Romans in time became enthusiastic sightseers and explorers. In our terms they became the tourists of the ancient world. It was explained to us at Ostia that the habit grew of setting up what we would call 'agencies' on the quayside at Ostia to serve all those travelling needs. Besides all that, as the Christian movement slowly gathered strength in the Roman Empire, a further new focus for pilgrimage to Jerusalem took over.

Talent spotting

The Musgrave Travelling Scholarship had been founded at Inst in 1923, so that by the time I came along about ten pupils had enjoyed its many benefits and had passed through the capable hands of Madame Dubois. It was therefore perfectly natural for Madame to recall the personalities of these boys and to talk about them to her summer guests.

I soon noticed that one name kept cropping up more often than any other – James, she simply called him. (Like most French speakers she had difficulty in pronouncing the harder 'dj' as in John or James, falling back on the more usual soft 'j' as the French do in Jacques or Jean. So James he remained, but no matter.) Apparently she and her friends had found James a most entertaining boy, a good storyteller, able to quote freely from French or English poetry and a mimic as well. She thought he would go far. In fact Madame Dubois had – in 1929, away down on the Bay of Biscay coast, identified a genuine talent that was to flourish in Belfast some twenty, thirty and forty years later as a much-loved schoolmaster at Inst, a versatile actor, a gifted reader of poetry, and a popular figure around the studios of BBC Radio where he was constantly in demand as a broadcaster.

Madame Dubois had spotted a star: James Boyce. Not only that, but he represented Northern Ireland in the national BBC Competition, 'Round Britain

Quiz', a few times during the 1950s.

Schleswig-Holstein

That title may confuse the reader and I mean it to do just that! I really wish to take the reader, in this memoir of mine, to Hamburg, the lovely open-air city with the smell of the sea all around and embellished by a chain of lakes – the Alster – running through the city centre. But the Province of Schleswig-Holstein must be disposed of first – at the isthmus, the junction of the Kingdom of Denmark with continental Germany.

Throughout the nineteenth century life in that province had been bedevilled by the confused state of the laws and practices of inheritance in matters of land, titles and power. So intricate had they become, so involved, so impenetrable, that it was widely accepted that no-one could understand them.

Joy came to the citizens when two learned men declared one day that, between them, they had found a solution and that the people could relax at long last. Joy turned to sorrow, however, when one of these two learned men went away and died. So great was the grief of his friend that he suffered a collapse and was forced to confess that he had forgotten his part of the solution! So we must leave the matter there and resume our travels.

Hamburg presented us with two attractive outlets

beyond the normal tourist zones. One was Bremen to the west, the home of Anna Töhl. Anna, a thoughtful and sensitive girl, had come to us earlier as an au pair helping to bring up our five little boys in Belfast. Getting to know Anna meant getting to know Anna's family in Bremen – mother Hedi, sister Ilse and brother Joachim. All became our friends, with us visiting Hedi in Bremen, Ilse taking up a position with our family in Belfast, and with Joachim and Helga visiting us at Milnthorpe, Cumbria (and watching avidly our television presentation of the wedding of Charles and Diana which happened to coincide with their stay).

In the other direction – that is to the east – we discovered an unusual seaside resort called Ostseebad Dahme (which I have described elsewhere in one of my short stories, '*Ein Korb, zwei Körbe*') when our son Myles was working there as a holiday worker in a restaurant run by a Frau Bishof.

Generally we found that these summer-month holiday jobs of our boys enriched our lives almost as much as they did theirs. The Blackpool trams, the English hop-farms, the Danish Royal Family farm, the Bromley Hotel, the Head Line Steamer carrying cargo and one or two passengers between Donegal Quay and Helsinki – all live with us yet in spirit.

A Conscientious Objector

Sending a few picture postcards from Madrid to

friends at home, I included one for my friend Robert whom I had got to know as an Assistant Secretary in the Whitehall Ministry of Health and later as a good neighbour in Westmorland. Apart from scribbling the usual message on my card to Robert, 'X marks the spot' and 'Wish you were here', I had paid little attention to the card itself and had not even noticed the picture of a minor sort of palace in the front.

On return home a week or so later we found a letter from Robert waiting for us – written in fluent Spanish and expressing much appreciation for my thoughtfulness in picking out and sending to him a picture of the very building in which he had spent World War II as a conscientious objector and as Manager of the Friends' Ambulance Unit.

Minnesänger

All through our married life Stella and I have had, looking down on us from the wall, a set of little colourful paintings of mediaeval figures – some of the *Minnesänger* of the twelfth century. Our favourite is Walther von der Vogelweide, born about 1170. He sang of love and, like other poets, singers and players of that enlightened century, Walther wandered a lot through Europe. In our flights of fancy we see him still travelling off the beaten track, on highways and byways, warming the hearts of men, women and children in his language of *Mittel-hoch-deutsch*. We cherish the vague hope that he will remember us and pay us a friendly visit one day.

East Prussia

Access from Königsberg to the seaside and countryside in East Prussia was easy. We made plenty of trips to Pillau, Kranzen and Rauschen to shudder in the ice-cold water of the Baltic, perhaps looking for a lucky find of amber or, more often, exploring every *Nehrung* and every *Haff* – a 'Nehrung' being a long narrow spit of land enclosing a lagoon, a 'Haff' being the lagoon itself – all rich in bird-life. This was one habitat where the cry of the lapwing – or the peewit as we called it – reminded us tenderly of home.

The loyal, patriotic students sharing our student lodgings at Oberteichufer insisted that Jack Crook and I go with them on a visit – or rather a solemn pilgrimage – to Tannenberg, the impressive but oversized monument to the German victory over the Russians in the early years of World War I.

Far more welcome and enjoyable was the friendly gesture of one student – the heir to a large horse-breeding Prussian estate at Pfaffendorf, Kreis Ortelsburg, asking me to spend *Pfingsten* with him on the home farm. This turned out to be the real thing – an essentially Junker establishment in deepest grassland country and run on the traditional lines of severe discipline and strict exclusiveness. On our first morning after breakfast my friend took me out into the stable yard where a group of silent workers were attending to their horses. Searching frantically for a vocative plural with which to address those men (grammar always obsessed me on such occasions, such a well-brought up schoolboy was I), I blurted out with well-intentioned gesture, *'Ich wünsche euch einen guten Morgen, meine Herren'*, only to be openly rebuked by my friend, 'We don't say anything like that here. These are not gentlemen. They are serfs.' Unfortunately he neglected to suggest to me any more acceptable form of greeting, so that over the seventy years since then I have fretted mildly on the point: would *Männer* have been better? Or *Freunde* or *Brüder* or *Genosse* or *Kamaraden* or *Burschen* or *Kerle*? How should one address some stable lads on a Junker estate in East Prussia under the eagle-eyed virulent Nazi supervisors? It now seems clear to me that *Heil Hitler* might have been grammatically, socially and politically the safest formula – but not from me.

Experience on that estate encouraged me to go still further into the country on my own and to get to know the Masurische lakes, a chain of freshwater lakes of ineffable beauty reflecting the great open sky of both Prussia and nearby Poland. I recognized the lakes later when I saw them appear in that charming Polanski film, *Knife in the Water*.

F.D. Squire of Inst, a splendidly fluent German speaker who influenced me greatly, was staying at that time with his family in Danzig. Along came a lovely invitation for Crook and me to join their party at Zoppot to see a performance of Gounod's *Faust* at the open-air opera house there.

Throughout one semester in Königsberg I had the benefit of having Jack Crook as a colleague companion and helper. A Lancashire lad, speaking with a strong Lancashire accent and the son of Lancastrian parents employed as specially recruited workers for some of the more refined techniques of cotton and linen manufacture at Muckamore Mill, he was just what I needed – practical, handy, reliable, resourceful as a student – just as he became an indispensable schoolmaster and head of cricket at Dungannon Royal School in adult life. I could not have had a better friend. I feel it right to include this little tribute for the sake of Jack's descendants today, wherever they may be in the world, if they read these memoirs.

To spare the reader any waste of time, let me explain that Königsberg is not only off the beaten track but off the map entirely. It no longer exists and has been replaced as 'Kaliningrad', now a city and port of Russia.

Russian Orthodox

Familiarity with Russian and Bulgarian male voice

choirs and with Russian short stories had prepared us to some extent for going into Russian churches, but not entirely. The shock is considerable. Stella and I first met it in Moscow where we visited several; so impressed were we that we later sought out and visited churches of the Russian Orthodox faith in many cosmopolitan cities of Europe and North America and in London as well. The first impression is of intensity – with much decoration from floor to ceiling, the brightest of colours, icons of sacred images painted on wood, heavy incense and much else – all far removed from our Ulster-Scot Presbyterian barn churches devoid of any decoration or images, and far also from our simple Quaker Meeting houses. There were no chairs or seats for the congregation, only stalls for the Czar and other aristocracy.

The next impression is of Eastern Art and Eastern influence throughout the whole system. Then, if we were fortunate, the thrilling tones of a live male voice choir at first hand. Here was a whole culture, language and faith available to us without having to travel another inch, for we found the churches often in the very street we were visiting anyway. It was to be abroad where we were already abroad. A metaphysical twist in the sense of travel, deep in the Russian psyche. All the time, of course, here was Christian worship being practised before our very eyes and ears, albeit in a strange idiom.

Sochi

Stella and I knew quite well that we were running a risk in planning to travel to Soviet Russia under the care of some small little-known travel agency in 1962, at a time of maximum Communist power and international tourism in the context of the Cold War. Russia was new to the tourist circuit, highly sensitive to criticism, slight or offence. There was every risk of becoming involved in some dubious situation and, as a result, losing our passports, being arrested, being put on trial, and even of being murdered under some pretext or other. Naturally we took commonsense precautions. As a further safeguard I had written to a friend in the diplomatic service who sent me, by return of post, a handy vade-mecum for people like us, written in his own hand on half a sheet of notepaper.

A voyage by Russian ship from Tilbury to Leningrad, under a woman captain and a woman chief engineer, a week in Leningrad followed by another week in Moscow and back again by rail to London, would have seemed to most sensible people to be quite enough for one holiday. We saw matters differently. Having negotiated the whole paraphernalia of passport, visa, foreign exchange, health cover and so on, surely, we argued, it would be only sensible to go the extra mile and see more of the country. So we tacked onto our planned journey an extra week at Sochi on the Black Sea. And to pile on the logic, we might never again have such a chance in this uncertain world. The nuclear bomb threatened us all, then.

Sochi impressed us for what it was intended to be and for what it actually was: a specially developed resort to accommodate approved Communist workers in planned holiday rooms. The reality bore this out. A little Moscow, to some extent, complete with *borscht* and *blini* but mercifully without *kvass*, that nauseous liquor made from fermented bread and served from small tankers on the streets of the capital.

One tiny incident opened our eyes to the question of class distinction that we were assured no longer existed in the Workers' Republic. On setting off for a bathe one morning in the waters of the Black Sea under the care of our young guide – and it would be utterly ungracious of us if we failed to recognize the professional skill of such guides in Russia at that time – the linguistic abilities, the efficiency, the alertness, their knowledge of their subject, their persistence in keeping in touch with their bosses, be they next door or away in Moscow – we proved over and over again that as a trained professional group the Russian Intourist women guides were splendid. Too splendid, perhaps. Catching a glimpse of a well-used beach where jolly crowds were enjoying themselves and where ladies were happily swimming in their underclothes, we slipped away from our tightly controlled group with the idea of sharing the fun at this spot. 'Come back! Come back! That is City Beach and you must not use it. You must use the first-class beach where I am taking you.' We gave in, of course, and the guide won in this battle of the classes – the classes being the ordered ranks of bureaucracy in the Soviet system.

Walking along a street in Sochi we were accosted politely by a Russian gentleman who fired at us a fast torrent of Russian. Now, every schoolboy knows that no matter how hard he has worked at his grammar book, in French let us say, or how many irregular verbs he can decline in the classroom, it is a very different matter when he is confronted by a real Frenchman in a real, live French situation. Fortunately I had been taking lessons in Russian from a splendid BBC television programme and had learned to recognize the sound of a few phrases such as *Cherno More* (The Black Sea) and *Mor Voksal* (Marine Station). The latter had for years amused both my wife and me for the surprising way in which Peter the Great had totally adopted the London district of Vauxhall to create their word for a railway station!!

I was thus just able to grasp that my Russian man simply wanted directions for getting to the harbour on the Black Sea where the public transport operated. Repeating loudly his own key phrases and making full strategic use of *levy* and *pravy* (left and right), as well as those two indispensable Russian syllables so well known across the political world, *da* and *nyet,* I managed to satisfy my man and leave him – with as much astonishment at getting the information as I felt at giving it – crying out, '*Spasibo, spasibo!*'

A German Biology

The excursions into the countryside from Berlin were totally unusual and probably unprecedented and unrepeated. They occurred in 1936 and 1937 during my bursary year at Bonn University. The German authorities, realizing what damage they were doing by their own totalitarian control of the economy, became anxious on seeing German students debarred from travelling abroad, from buying books and journals from the West, and generally losing touch with education and science in the Western World, save under their own most severely controlled conditions. So they devised a scheme for a type of residential, high-pressure tutorial at which – publicly – the tutors would be fellows like me but – secretly – with visiting experts lecturing us all on what amounted to Fascist propaganda of the higher sort.

One such tutorial was in the Spreewald just southeast of Berlin and managed under firm Nazi control with truly Spartan standards of accommodation and food. The lectures inflicted on us were unbelievably crude

– the need of the German *Volk* for a thoroughly German type of biology, for instance, leading on, no doubt, to plans for a pure Aryan race and so forth, and much rubbish of the same kind. And, significantly again, the need for a German history so as to tell the world how much Germany had suffered over the centuries. For those of us interested in the workings of the Nazi mind, here was enlightenment in the raw, to be had at first hand. I found it all so boring that I quickly put it out of my mind.

The second attempt – they must have imagined that I was a usable tool or something, for they pressed me to attend again – took place in the German Ruhrland, the centre of the flourishing arms industry. We were allowed one evening out on the town that proved to be memorable for reasons which the organisers had not foreseen – visiting a theatre in Bochum where a play was being presented on a silently revolving stage, a triumph of German engineering in those days of 1937.

Apfelstrudel

The idea of a holiday on one or other of the famous Italian lakes – Garda, Como or Maggiore – might seem pleasure enough, but on our first visit there we were impressed also by the proximity of towns with such German names as Meran and Bozen rather than anything Italian-sounding.

Going into a post office with my little bit of Italian language ready for action, I was taken aback to hear the clerk greet us with '*Guten Morgen; was möchten Sie?* Here was an Italian post office, operating under the Italian state, in Italy, but run in the German language. This was obviously a remnant of the old Austrian-Hungarian Empire, which used to cross the Alps and occupy much of what we now know as Italy.

The surprise to me – someone who had been interested in the pattern of settlements after Versailles – was to find the German language still surviving in what seemed to be settled and undisputed land. This contradicted the prediction I had been making for years to the effect that, with universal radio and television, such oddities of surviving languages in strange places would surely be ironed out gradually, and that for official purposes we would be moving towards a reduced quota of principal languages in the world – English, French, Spanish, Chinese perhaps. Not so; here was German – not exactly the easiest language to learn – surviving in the Italian North fully as well as their delicious *Apfelstrudel* itself.

Of course the position is by no means unique to North Italy. It is well known to be repeated in many quarters – French and Flemish in Belgium, French and English in Montreal, and so on – indeed, if anything, the tide of the current is running in the other direction, in the sense that there are many examples of minor languages claiming and achieving recognition. One good example is Ullans in Northern Ireland, previously looked on as merely a dialect of Ulster Scots but now accepted as a minor language in its own right. Although not a convinced enthusiast for Ullans as a language, I confess I did contribute my little bit to its development as a spoken and written dialect. Although this growing number of 'recognized languages' can complicate life for politicians and administrators and can drive up costs, it appears to be a fact – welcomed by some, resisted by others – which we must live with.

Kehl

It was as interesting for Simon as for us – if not even more so – to be in Strasbourg and to see for ourselves to what extent the city and the whole province of Alsace had successfully reverted to French language, culture and habits after fifty years of government by Germany – that is, from the end of the Franco-Prussian War in 1870 until the end of the World War II in 1945. While we were merely on a visit from home, Simon had come from Berlin in around 1960 where he had been living and working for many years and so had to make even greater adjustments than we had.

While we were observing that French was all around us on the streets, we spotted an ordinary country bus with the shortest of destination boards: Kehl. It took us on a pleasant but tedious journey – out of France, across an international frontier through all the many formalities, with showing of passports, visas and the changing of currencies under supervision of a French military guard, over the River Rhine, into Germany – to the small town of Kehl and to a café where we could read *Die Süddeutsche Zeitung* and enjoy the best of Würtemberg's *Kaffee* and *Schwarzwälder Kirschtorte*.

As other German customers joined us we all indulged in communal sadness at the poor showing of the football team Bayern-München in the previous few matches. All I could contribute was an assurance, off the cuff, that the team would never fail so long as they had as goalkeeper that young man who could do no wrong, Oliver Kahn, who hails from Karlsruhe in the Baden province just up the road.

A German Spa

The administration and the legislation in Northern Ireland form part of a 'devolved government' and are strictly confined to the scope and limit of the functions transferred to it by superior authority in London. But such a restriction does not preclude us from observing what happens in the rest of the United Kingdom or in the Irish Republic or in Europe, taking an interest in such matters and learning from them. I go one step further, arguing that we should always be on the lookout for an opportunity to let the wider world know of any development of ours that might be of interest to them.

As it happened, in the 1950s, we were managing to rationalize and modernize the law relating to rent restriction, well known to lawyers as a difficult and intricate code of law. When this came to the knowledge of a body in West Germany, Die Deutsche Bau und Boden Bank, they got in touch with us. The outcome was an invitation to me to visit them to address a conference of top representatives in Germany of the building industry – architects, town planners, lawyers, financiers and others.

The venue was the delightful spa town of Bad Homburg in the hills outside Frankfurt am Main, housing the most elegant conference facilities imaginable. Clearly the address had to be in the German language, and pretty good German at that, to satisfy such an audience. I found the task of preparation extremely hard work, not only for the formal address itself but also in readiness for the inevitable session of question and answer that was bound to follow.

Two years later I was asked to go again, this time to speak on slum clearance and redevelopment –

another brutally difficult field to cover in German. A third invitation came two years later; this time the topic which had caught the interest of the German building fraternity was the story of the British new towns. For this, the third time, I laboured hard to meet the needs of the situation. Why? Courtesy, to begin with. As I had been so courteously invited, a courteous response was called for. Secondly, I had come to know many of the German people concerned and was glad to support them in their post-war revival. But somehow, overall, I felt a strong call of duty – duty to seize this chance of helping to put Northern Ireland on the map of Europe and thus of strengthening our position and our standing. My three papers were subsequently printed and thus became part of the permanent record of the people and the bodies concerned.

Nowadays I argue in favour of other parts of the Northern Ireland administration taking every chance to look beyond their extremely narrow legal limits on subjects which would, I am sure, carry much more interest and attraction than those which I was dealing with – veterinary research, grassland development, animal health control, and to 'sell' our more desirable goods in other words.

France D.I.Y.

By about 1961 Stella and I had decided that it was

time our boys paid a visit to France and learned something of French life and customs. Julian, aged seventeen, was beginning to drop out of family holidays, so that left Stella and me plus four others – Marcus, Simon, Myles and Quintin. We were determined to make our own arrangements, to go exactly where we wanted and when. Some families take their children abroad at an early age, fondly believing that even to see a shop with a sign *'Patisserie'* above the door was an education in itself! As we wanted a lot more than that, we picked a year when the ages ranged from fifteen to six.

We started by making an arrangement with SNCF to give us one composite travel ticket covering Paris, Blois and Les Sables d'Olonne. That worked well and saved us a lot of headaches and minor crises. Then we had the good fortune to have had my friend Mlle Giraud in Belfast in connection with a function in her field of pharmacy at Queen's staying with us at Circular Road; in return she booked us into rooms close to where her mother and she lived, on the left bank of the Seine. The scene was thus set for an intense visit to Paris and all its attractions. One unexpected highlight was the gift to Stella and me of tickets for *La Cantatrice Chauve* by Ionesco in a basement theatre in the Rue de la Huchette (or was it 'La Rue du chat qui pêche'?). At any rate the actors spoke their lines at a rate approaching 400 words a minute, I reckoned.

For our stay in Blois on the River Loire we had arranged, long in advance and in carefully penned letters, to stay at Hotel Tourne-bride where we opened the eyes of our boys by sharing the breakfast room with the council dustmen. There was much to see in connection with their famous local men, Blaise Pascal and Denis Papin, as well as the Chateaux of the Loire; but we had decided to spend our time just living the life and enjoying the atmosphere of a French provincial town. We simply soaked ourselves in the air of the streets, the park, the river; and we contrived to make our boys do as much as possible of the daily shopping.

Les Sables d'Olonne was next – a resort on the Bay of Biscay with a splendid *plage* – one of few we found to rival our wonderful beaches in Ireland. Our modest hotel had the usual French emphasis – a kitchen and dining room but little else. The boys dealt with this themselves by getting involved in the workings of the place; one of their contributions was to collect all the empty breakfast trays and deliver them to the lower regions – earning the odd *croissant* on the way as they found that *le petit déjeuner* was a slight affair. This was all exactly what we wanted and needed: *Paris à la Plage*. All Paris seemed to have moved down on 14th July for the *vacances*. Good citizens from Montparnasse had fixed a rendezvous with their neighbours to meet here – with effusive greetings in high and mighty Parisian accents. A gentleman greeting a lady would remove his hat and gallantly hold it in his hand despite the blazing sun until his gracious family would cry out, '*Couvrez-vous, Monsieur, couvrez-vous!*'

Barbe à papa was all the rage – a hideous concoction of blown-up sugary pink foam – and, of course, *les glaces* in every imaginable shape and form. A pilgrimage was arranged to let the boys see the seaside house where Dad had spent his exciting travelling scholarship in 1932 – in St Giles-Croix de Vie, the neighbouring village.

Having had, for once, the good sense to keep a record of all the places we had been to, we made up a huge diary on the montage principle, into which went every metro ticket, hotel receipt, smart advertisement, snapshot and silly little reminder of happy carefree days, including a marvellous photo of an estate agent's office with his business notice '*Agence Fraud*', which was to win magazine prizes for us afterwards. The last page was cut out from *Le Figaro* and showed an empty beach with the deckchairs stacked and the motto '*Fin de Saison*'.

La rentrée was upon us all. In the summer of 2004 our French grandchildren arrived in England for their holiday, crying out as soon as they reached our flat, 'Where is the diary?' We were glad to oblige. For them it was already a piece of history.

Voltaire

Maurice Oldfield and I took the opportunity of a free day at the Zimmern School of International Studies to go the few miles from Geneva to Ferney in order to see the house where Voltaire had lived. We were lucky to find quickly the famous formula that he had devised as a guide to good government: 'Work dispels boredom, vice and poverty.'

Remarkable in its day for being so apt, so valid, so relevant and so succinct.

Then I stumbled on the details of Voltaire's imprisonment in the Bastille on account of his radical views. These were new to me. The simple truth was that I had, at the age of nineteen or twenty, raced at high speed through *Candide, Les Lettres Philosophiques,* and much else in order to be able to report that I had done my Voltaire, my J. J. Rousseau and others, but without bothering to notice anything about the problems, afflictions or imprisonment of this man, probably the sharpest mind in Europe in the eighteenth century. As usual, it was a verbal point that impressed me so much at the time – the use of the awful word 'bastille' as a verb: Voltaire had been *embastillé,* if you please. Perhaps there was some compensating irony to be felt when history showed that the Bastille, to which the *Ancien Régime* had cruelly sent Voltaire, proved to be the trigger that started the whole French Revolution of 1789, sweeping away that very *régime* itself.

France à la Carte

This amusing yet apt title, far from merely being a passing tribute to the glories of French cuisine, carries a more serious message. Simon and his partners in the business company of that name advise their customers to make their own arrangements for getting to France, for they know from experience that their customers will know the companies, the timings, the pricing and points of departure, and so on, that suit them best in their home countries. Within France they are then offered the fullest range of choice in the aspect of life and activity which interests them most: climbing, fishing, golf, music, sea bathing, the unique charm of Napoleon's Corsica (in which Simon is something of a specialist), literary associations, antiquities, archaeology or whatever. 'France à la carte' helps them to find the best arrangement. Simon's familiarity with local travel, politics and cultural affairs on the internet comes into play; so also does his fluency in modern French and German language; and of course his twenty years of practical experience of living, working, lecturing, interpreting and bringing up his own family in the total French situation.

Il n'y a qu'un Bonn

'*Il n'y a qu'un Bonn*', declared the post office clerk in Brussels as he struck out two of the words I had written on my telegram form: '*am Rhein*'. He was, of course, being perfectly correct and he was saving me a bit of money on the international telegram that I was proposing to send to my friends at Kronprinzenstrasse 7 to let them know of my travel plans, as I generally liked to do. And yet the clerk was inadvertently handing me a splendid piece of untarnished tourist publicity, 'There is only one Bonn.' What could be better?

In all my experience I had found few small towns that could surpass Bonn as a city of beauty, distinction and presence. From time to time one heard mutterings of small-mindedness amongst landladies gossiping about their student boarders, but that did nothing to take away from the general dignity and standing of the city.

Situated on the left bank of the River Rhine – that is the west bank – Bonn carries on the tradition laid down by the Romans two thousand years earlier. Having dealt with Iberia and Gaul (divided into three parts, of course), the Romans wisely contented themselves with occupying and developing that bank – Cologne, Trier, Coblenz and Bonn – stopping short of crossing the big river and engaging with those strange Germanic tribes reputed to occupy the dark forests and swamps over there.

Bonn, though still not a big town, can claim to have much in its favour today: the Münster (cathedral), the university, many learned institutions, that great bookshop of Röhrscheid, easy access by land westward into France, north along the left bank, up and down the big river by boat. Most towns have a town square, but Bonn has three: Münsterplatz, Marktplatz and Kaiserplatz. Fine streets ranging from Koblenzerstrasse running under the Koblenzertor to Mauspfad in the old town centre; and Poppelsdorfer Allee surely ranking with the great streets of Europe. Some features have been surprisingly well preserved – the unbroken quadrangle of cloisters at the Münster, for example, or the wide handsome Hofgarten of unspoilt lawn directly before the university itself, that has set it off so magnificently for artists and photographers for generations past and has miraculously been saved from sacrifice to political and commercial demands. And, of course, it boasts the birthplace of Beethoven – an example of eighteenth-century beauty and distinction – and, to my taste, of utter simplicity.

Adaptable, too, this small town was called on after World War II to act as capital, seat of government and headquarters of national administration as well as diplomatic headquarters for West Germany until the two Germanys were united again. I learned from friends in the departments there that when the decision was finally taken to make Berlin capital of the reunified country there were many in Bonn hesitant or even unwilling to make the move up to graceless Berlin from their beloved, intimate, graceful Bonn. Incidentally, I had been one of those who had playfully argued in favour of adopting as patron saint none other than Saint Boniface.

In line with my general approach in these memoirs I must mention, only to dismiss, a multitude of interesting or attractive villages and other settlements around Bonn that I would otherwise be concentrating on. There are too many and they are all too well known and visited already. The region is rich in history and in literary associations. Beuel just across the river by the Kennedy Bridge – there you have a heap of political interest at a stroke; the Doppelkirche (one church built on top of another); Mehlem with a ferry service that saves you many kilometres of road; Königswinter, a sophisticated resort since Victorian times; the Siebengebirge, Germany's first nature reserve; the Drachenfels where Siegfried slayed the dragon. Back across the Rhine is Bad Godesberg where Hitler slayed Chamberlain's dragon, so to speak; the Venusberg; Poppelsdorf; and down the beautiful Allee. All too well known and now lacking that spark of individuality that I am seeking.

We must go down the Rhine a little, still on the left bank, halfway to Cologne where we find the rococo Schloss Brühl. Here are Bonn and the Rhineland at their best: the ambitious programme of Beethoven's Nine Symphonies being played in one Beethoven *Woche* in delightful surroundings by leading orchestras; the most attentive and informal audience, and supper accompanied by a *Pfirsich*

Bowle, Rhine wine with saturated white peaches floating in it.

Or a second choice. This time up-river, still on the left bank, by rail to the little town of Boppard lying on a long, wide curve of the river where one can watch, with great advantage, that eternal source of human interest – the tugboat dragging a string of barges on their way from Basel to Rotterdam. Has the captain remembered to bring his bicycle with him and lash it to a post on deck? Or is that his car I see on deck this time? And has his good wife had enough time this morning to get her domestic washing strung out on the line?

Boppard springs another surprise by being the world centre for the design and trade in bent-wood furniture. A literally unique museum houses bent-wood furniture in an astonishing range of articles – not only the traditional hat-stand – including the very article that we had in our house in Belfast in the 1920s I do believe – but also a cradle and lots more that we must take a chance of seeing another day.

Krupp at Essen and Belfast

1937 was a time of growing division in Britain over policy towards Germany. The National Socialist Party (NSDP) had quickly established its grip on the whole German administration and there were signs everywhere of a revival of German aggression and domination. Some of our leaders, like Churchill, were predicting war and were urging immediate rearmament. Others, like Chamberlain, foresaw the threat of war equally clearly but were unwilling to take steps that would plunge Britain and her allies needlessly into the horrors of worldwide war, of which they had all too vivid memories. All this time Germany was rearming fast; and rearming meant intense activity by the family-dynasty of Krupp at Essen.

Here was I, a British student of German language, life and culture, living in Germany and close to the very scene of the action both political and military. My puritan upbringing began to tell me that it was time I took notice, for I had been living a life of comparative ease and comfort, making happy weekend trips to different parts of the country, admiring pretty villages and joining in useless intellectual discussions with contemporaries at those delightful universities of Tübingen, Erfurt and Marburg.

Krupp at Essen represented the harsh reality, let there be no doubt. As would only be expected, I had by then built up quite a company of good friends in Germany, decent citizens, one would say, by any standard. As well as the long-term friendships with the Winternheims in Königsberg and the Breuers in Bonn, I had my more recent colleagues in the Deutsche Bau und Boden Bank, all those nice girls who had helped us in Belfast as au pair guests, along with their supportive families, and in the normal course of events, in every corner of the land, decent men and women whom I liked and whose acquaintance I valued. One of the latest that I got to know in my last months there was a Jewish family – a most cultured family – living discreetly in a nondescript flat somewhere between Bonn and Godesberg in the diplomatic quarter. Their opulent rooms, rich in books, pictures, music and original artistic treasures from distant parts always meant an experience for me; and the children seemed glad to have 'an Englishman' around.

While I did not for a moment imagine that I could play any positive role at that stage, I knew that I ought at the very least to go and see Essen for myself. Essen was one of the main centres of the Ruhrland, the well-established industrial area lying just north of Cologne. I had been to Düsseldorf. I had been greatly impressed and even threatened by the evident strength of Duisberg, lying at the confluence of the Rivers Rhein and Ruhr, and claiming to be the busiest river port in Europe.

Arriving in Essen I had no difficulty in identifying the Krupp presence for it dominated the city and was surrounded by a high protective wall some three or four metres high. Where better to spend a wet Saturday than trudging round those walls, let us say ten kilometres of them, as part of my act of personal penance? I had to force my way through the factory workers coming and going off duty, as well as ordinary citizens on their normal Saturday business.

To be clear, I had no mission. I had no plan for saving the world. Krupp were stoking up the fires of war and I just wanted to be there and to see what I could see. Which of course was not very much – Krupp had seen to that. The place was a formidable fortress. Still, it pleased me to be able to peer through any little opening in the wall or any gatepost. Towards the end of my dreary walk one opening was appearing where the wall had to allow an industrial canal to emerge and where I could look in and clearly see model aircraft suspended in mid-air, aircraft parts in the making, and articles that might very well be bombs in the act of being stacked for transport to some airfield, for there was obviously no room for an airfield or landing strip at this place. I could see the fearsome pattern. As I plodded on, muttering old proverbs and sayings to myself, I knew that I was being seen by the guards but no-one took any notice of me, judging me to be some harmless crank.

All that was in the Spring of 1937. Four years later the Luftwaffe dropped their bombs on Belfast, aiming at the shipyard and the harbour where the American troops first set foot in Europe when America joined in the war. Alas, some of the German bombs missed those strategic targets and fell on the residential areas that enfold them. During one raid in April six hundred men, women and children were killed, and in May two hundred more. To me personally it seemed quite likely that those bombs, as well as the flares which eerily preceded them and the incendiary bombs which were carefully timed to accompany them, had been manufactured by Krupp within those high walls that I had come to know in Essen.

The impact on me was even more direct when, acting as duty officer in charge of our Civil Defence Operations Room at Stormont Castle, I had to note down and record the information sent up to me by our trained Observer Corps on the make and origin of one spent explosive after another. For a moment or two I thought of trying to link those armaments that I had seen in Essen with the bombs identified on the Shore Road or in Ballymacarrett, but the bigger situation was so tragic that I soon saw that this was neither the time nor the place to start playing such games. I got on with my work.

Corsica

Simon taught us more about the island of Corsica in the course of our two visits there than we could otherwise have learned in a lifetime. He was able to give us the benefit of his direct experiences as a driver and as an interpreter for French, German and English when he had got to know every corner of Corsica – not only the towns of Ajaccio, Bastia, Calvi and Bonifacio, but the villages, the coastline, the beauty spots and the politically dangerous spots as well. One night we three shared a three-bedded bedroom in a modest house in remote Zonza where I doubt many British visitors had ever stayed before. And, may I add, on both of our visits we suffered cold blustery weather in the month of May, when the wind literally drove us off the beaches.

Corsica, on the one hand an integral part of France and contributing two *départements* to the French administrative system, was on the other hand rent apart on political grounds between those who were then agitating for independence from France and those who were sticking loyally to the established regime. Violence was commonplace and discord was rife even within the schools.

I mention these experiences to exemplify the sort of unique help that a son or a daughter living and working in a region can give. In Simon's case his advice and assistance ranged over a much wider field on the many occasions when we stayed with him in Toulouse. His easy relationship with schools, hospitals, restaurants, universities, chambers of commerce, tourist offices – as well as his constant battle to be allowed to vote in some elections – all combined to let us see the French way of life at close range. Add Sylvie's wide family connections in the

Castres Albi area. All the time you are in the heart of true rugby-playing country, if you are interested.

The French system of government-approved *gîtes* opened up further pleasures; Simon's familiarity with the system let him get the best bookings for us. It is only right to record that we found the cottages good but not universally wonderful. The real gain was in getting to know the villages, the home bakeries and so on, as well as in enjoying walks and picnics high up in the Pyrenees.

There is, alas, a sad side to all this as well, namely the decline in the French village, the death indeed of many a village deserted in favour of the bigger towns. The parallel with the situation in England was obvious, where we are exhorted to support the village post office, for example, on the lines of 'use it or lose it'.

The national elections, the European referendum, the switch to the Euro coinage, the launch of the great new innovative aeroplane at Blagnac, the horrible explosion of a chemical factory – we feel part of what is going on in France, either through the family or through the local newspaper which Simon sends us from time to time and which we then hand on to the Arnside butcher, M. Poteau, who is a Toulousain.

Munich

In the same sort of way Myles, living and working in

the city of Munich, old and modern at the same time, with its push-button transport and its extraordinary wealth of bookshops, libraries, and theatres of every kind, takes us well into the life of the present-day city. A typical scene in Myles's household in the middle of that great city is to see him draw from his pocketbook a tiny little press cutting about some performance by a local scholar, poet or wit being held in an obscure basement theatre which I would otherwise never have heard of but which he had long in advance carefully noted for our benefit – something in rapid, quick-fire German that will test me to the limit, but which helps to keep me up-to-date.

Always ready and prepared to play his part in making our visits memorable, Myles has taken us to lots of places between Munich and the Alps. The Munich people take a particular pride in explaining that their city is so well-placed that at the end of the tramlines the Alps begin and a wonderful panorama opens out for every motorist, ski-runner and cyclist, with facilities at hand for renting the necessary gear. Myles's tally is impressive and he has made sure that we have got to know Berchtesgaden, the Königsee, Garmisch-Partenkirchen, Mittenwald (the centre of the violin-making industry), Oberammergau and a lot more. One highlight consisted in booking us in to a bed-and-breakfast place in the delightful Alpbach, away off the Inn Valley in Tyrol, where we thought the atmosphere and the cuisine were about the lightest and brightest anywhere we had come across in Europe. We can attest that they give the lie to that tired old accusation about German hospitality always being dull, heavy and uninspired. No way.

Always keen to bring off a surprise coup carefully chosen and devised to meet the predilections of his parents, Myles surpassed himself in 1985 by organizing a great family Christmas party at Deggendorf and inviting everyone. Stella and I reached Deggendorf by train, having travelled fast via Landshut, where we watched the well-turned-out and punctilious stationmaster wave on our train at the very moment the red hand on the huge station clock reached the exact top of its dial. We had time to enjoy some delicious *Apfelpfankuchen* at the station café in Deggendorf before the others arrived, as the German railway can generally be counted on to serve splendid station fare in all parts of the country – north, south, east or west.

By now we were at the extreme eastern edge of Germany, right up against the Czech border and in deep forest country – the Bohemian Forest – heavily coated with snow and ice. We were in magical village life at once. Midnight mass by moonlight at the forest church. Our people kept coming from all directions – Leni with her style and elegance up and down the little village street provided the local residents with gossip for a twelve-month period afterwards, they told us.

Global Warming

The travel topic with which I close these memoirs has a surprising relationship with one of the great obsessions of our times. It may even possibly have been of help in trying to foretell the coming of that phenomenon. If a minor heatwave could have the effect described here, how much more could a major heatwave have?

Everybody knows that the German language favours long, composite nouns made up of built-in segments. Simple examples are: for a pram read *Kinderwagen*; for a tool read *Handwerkzeug*. Even the familiar *Kindergarten* is another example. I found an example that came closest to real life in a most spectacular, scribbled emergency notice at a River Rhine landing stage during a short hot spell. I noted it down with pen and paper and it read like this, all in one word:

Kölndüsseldorfrheindampferniedrigwasserzustandsonderfahrplan

Part II

Come Far Away With Me

A Briefing In Congress

My first visit to America took place in 1972 and came as a total surprise. At a time of serious trouble and great uncertainty in Ulster the United States Congress had decided to hold a series of hearings into the Ulster Question. I was despatched at short notice to travel to Washington to brief Senators and House Representatives single-handedly on the facts of the situation before they began hearing the politicians and other witnesses, and to answer the questions that worried them.

Rather than compose an account now, I am simply reproducing an extract from the notes I made shortly afterwards, in order to convey to readers a more immediate sense of how public business can develop and how a public official like me has to respond. In line with the spirit of these memoirs it is once more a tale of travel laced with human interest.

A Centre of Excellence

Earl Mountbatten of Burma was waiting for us by the runway of Valleta Airport ready to receive us to Malta on the first leg of our Foreign Tour. Not wanting to overburden my account of this monumental journey with too many names I confine myself to mentioning Lord Mountbatten, former Head of Combined Operations in HM Forces and last Viceroy of India, in order to indicate right away the sort of top-level arrangement under which we were travelling. We were a group of fifteen students from one of the leading military colleges in England, representing the Navy, Army and Air Force and Civil Service of Britain and six Commonwealth countries, all around the age of forty and ranking Naval Captain, Brigadier, Air Commodore and Assistant Secretary.

Since it was set up as a school of international studies for senior officers of the services the college had gradually and empirically developed some sound practices: placing civil servants alongside service officers; mixing officers from the different forces in every activity, including, later on, men from the United States of America; encouraging all to study international affairs at depth and from many different angles, each student sharing with the others his particular knowledge or experience in a sort of unspoken, quasi-tutorial rôle; and relying on a library unusually well-stocked with up-to-date publications from all over the world. My field was easily defined as that of Health and Social Services, as it happened that I had been helping to prepare legislation on social subjects as well as lecturing to Workers' Educational students at evening classes in disused Nissan huts around Belfast, and all the time studying in my chilly bedroom with a blanket round my knees in preparation for some work I was doing on a 'Philosophical Analysis of the Presuppositions and Implications of the Welfare State'. The University thought it good enough to merit a PhD. Afterwards my three Professorial Tutors and the External Examiner reckoned it must have been the first such study in the world.

Getting back to the quality of the college itself, its standard can be judged by a statement made publicly by a commandant in 2004: 'The college is offering a unique and enriching experience the like of which is simply not available anywhere else in the world.' Little wonder, then, that the college earned for itself (and has managed to keep) the enviable description as a 'centre of excellence'.

From a carefully balanced programme of work I have decided to pick one item only for inclusion in these memoirs of travel: the foreign tour. Fully briefed in advance from diplomatic sources; on a planned itinerary of Asia and Africa; with clear aims stated; in a plane specially placed at our disposal by the RAF and manned by an RAF crew; in constant telecommunication contact with our base and with the next stopping place; under arrangements that let us be received and looked after by the president, prime minister or commander-in-chief of each country visited: such was the situation.

Malta, then, to start with. Next Egypt and the Suez Canal zone where we spent time with a battalion of a Guards regiment, drilling in the sand, as we saw. On to two stations in the Persian Gulf, Bahrain and Sharja, where we did what we could to help keep up the morale of the dozen or so of our British soldiers manning a lonely outpost of empire in what could only be described as vile conditions of heat and humidity. Then up over Mesopotamia to Baghdad where the temperature was 117° F and where I burned my hands by thoughtlessly grasping the metal hand-rail of the gangway of our plane.

When I remonstrated slightly over these conditions and over the speed with which we had to move from one base to the next, I was met with the reply, 'One day you will be a top person sent out on an urgent mission to some hot country surrounded by wars and rumours of wars, by diseases and rumours of diseases, told to complete your mission and report back home within 72 hours. So, young man, get yourself ready now!'

Aden was our last port of call in Asia, later subsumed into South Yemen, now Yemen. Then over the Red Sea to Africa – north, south, east and west

– on a remarkable programme of intense variety and interest. Somaliland; Ethiopia the homeland of the ancient Kingdom of Judah, reaching right back to the time of King David in the Bible some 10,000 years earlier; Sudan. Then the three East African states of Kenya, Uganda and Tanganyika. In Kenya a safari into the country of the great wild beasts had been arranged, to show us something of the eternal problem of managing and living with wildlife. I declined, arguing primly that that was not my scene; but when I had been persuaded to change my mind and take part, I found myself the most enthusiastic watcher of them all, in a situation of incomparable beauty and danger, with the closest possible view of giraffe, eland, tiger and elephant, as well as the king of the jungle himself, waking up before our very eyes and ears to his day's imperious activity.

Further south, then, to Southern Rhodesia which I greatly admired, where I thought I would willingly have stayed and where the man in charge of electoral arrangements was a County Londonderry man. As it happened, all the talk, there and then, was of the negotiations taking place in preparation for a new vision of Africa: a Central African Federation comprising Southern Rhodesia, Northern Rhodesia (Zambia) and Nyasaland (Malawi) that seemed to hold some promise and could possibly have formed a strong force for good in Darkest Africa. Local rivalries, alas, frustrated all efforts and the vision vanished.

Mindful of the economic realities of all this, our directing staff had laid much emphasis in our programme on the productive farming of Southern Rhodesia (now Zimbabwe) and on the copper mining of Northern Rhodesia. In an effort at conveying to a wider public a realistic picture of the daily life in those parts, I have since then included two short stories, 'Kisses for the Voters' and 'The Burden of the White Man', in my book *Personalities at Poppelsdorf* published in 1991.

Homeward by way of West Africa – so different from all the rest of the continent. In particular Nigeria and the Gold Coast (later Ghana), where colourful life stretches from the impressive coastline on the Gulf of Guinea in the south right up to the Muslim part bordering on the Sahara desert. The impact of noise, activity and colour struck us forcibly, especially the sight of the mammy-wagons, open lorries crammed with women being transported to and from those thriving markets run by the women themselves.

It was in one of our planned talks that I felt most keenly something of the dangers brewing in Africa. Without doubt it was an exceptional privilege to be able to discuss with the most senior representatives of each country in turn the essence of their political concerns, as well as their hopes and fears in matters of defence, all in an atmosphere of confidence and mutual trust. But having to listen to some self-appointed and bombastic general, laden with medals, while he tried to impress us with stories of grandiose structures, statues and symbols being built at huge expense under financial arrangements that would satisfy no self-respecting auditor, I found myself unable to remain silent and, instead, obliged to speak up: 'Yes, sir, all very well but surely what your country needs, from what little we have seen, is much more money and effort being devoted to the things that really make a stable and civilized society: more police constables, sanitary officers, health visitors, food inspectors, nurses, midwives, primary school teachers, auditors and the like.' He changed the subject.

Our last stopping-place was Timbuktu, capital of Mali in mid-Sahara.

Gathering my thoughts together now, I hope that it may be more helpful to readers if instead of tacking on to each section of these memoirs a word or two of my personal opinion, which readers may or may not want to hear, I finish this whole work with a frank avowal of the overall position in public affairs which experience has led me to adopt and from which the readers can make their own judgments.

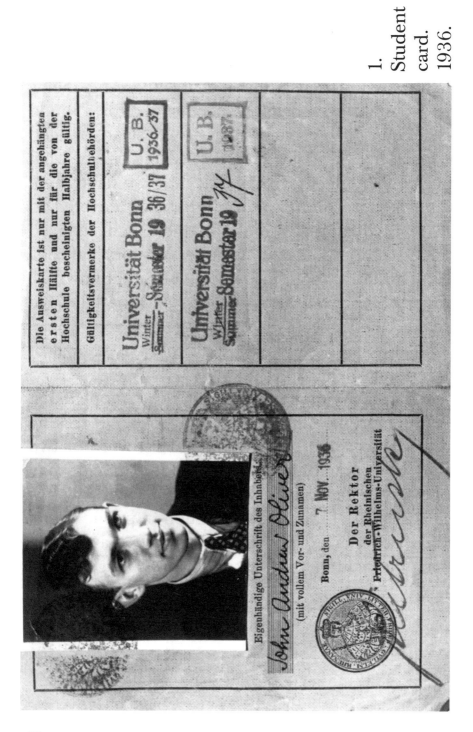

1. Student card. 1936.

2. The parents. 1904.

3. John and his four sisters and two brothers. Belfast, 1984.

4. Quintin, Julian, Simon, Marcus, Myles. 2004.

5. The Magilligan Cottage, moved stone by stone to the Ulster Folk and Transport Museum, Cultra. With appreciation and thanks.

6. The Hezlett House, built 1691 at Castlerock, Coutny Londonderry. By courtesy of the National Trust. With appreciation and thanks.

7. We kept in touch.

8. Stella with John. London, 2002.

9. Mary Robinson, President of the Republic of Ireland with Quintin, one of her advisors.

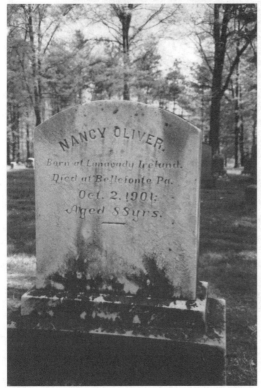

10. Head stone, Nancy Oliver. Nancy was a valuable link in the American connection. Pennsylvania, USA, 1813–1901.

11. Minnesänger from the 12th or 13th Century

Part III

Back to the Family Homeland

The Northern Ireland Perspective

When I consulted my sons (all of whom were born and educated in Ulster) on the hand-written early drafts, they were quick to point out two serious gaps in the structure of these memoirs: first, that whereas I had described some twenty or thirty places that I had visited in my travels abroad, I had not even mentioned Northern Ireland (or Ulster as we usually call it) which was my homeland and theirs and with which I might be expected to be familiar; the second gap related to the fact that, although I had touched on some important matters of public interest, I had never revealed my personal opinions. I understand both those lines of criticism and am ready to deal with them in my own way.

My Method

This work is *not* a diary with everyday dates all accounted for, still less is it a curriculum vitae with every stage of training and qualifying carefully recorded. It is simply a gather-up of essays or (as Dr Samuel Johnson, the great lexicographer would describe them) 'loose sallies of the mind'. It is through these essays that I have tried to convey my present memories of and reflections on travel stretching back to 1932. In the same way now, also, I hope to fill the second gap, not by adding a line or two to each section, but in a way that may throw a lot more light on the whole matter for the reader.

This may involve running the two problems together. There is a further advantage in running the two aspects in double harness. As my friend Professor Seamus Carney taught me, Ulster means essentially a people rather than a place. As he put it (none too elegantly), Ulster has always been, throughout history, 'a pair of bellows' – now expanding, now contracting with each change in political fortune. Ulster, the people, remains essentially the same whether at home or away; indeed scholars have often observed that the Ulsterman has the ability to exist in two places at once, as I believe I have been doing for a good part of my life.

Places of International Renown

All the world knows of the Giant's Causeway, that extraordinary composition of molten basalt cooled into hexagonal columns that always lent themselves so easily to the mythology of a Giant's Organ, a Giant's pathway, a Giant's Wishing Well, and so on. The lesser remnants of the same geological formation surviving on the Island of Staffa in Scotland simply demanded a belief in a causeway (or 'cassay' as we call it) linking the two ends for the convenience of mythical giants. Today the Giant's Causeway itself acts as Northern Ireland's premier tourist attraction.

In a similar way the Antrim Coast Road, carved out of the narrow strip of land between the cliffs and the sea, plays its part in attracting much international interest. The aspect which I have always appreciated most is the striking contrast between the black basalt overhanging the white chalk and, at points where it ceases to overhang, the blocks of vivid black and white enriching the scenery like – if I may say so – some Giant's Dice.

Not basalt this time but granite is what you get in the magnificent cluster of the Mourne Mountains in County Down. Apparently the grey-green granite, buried deeply, cooled more slowly in geological time and formed the recognizable large grain, while the black basalt was extruded into the sea and cooled more rapidly into tiny grains as a result – so far as I understand the science of these matters. Basalt and granite are therefore two of our most prominent topographical features.

'Derry's Walls', as they are popularly known,

represent another feature of international interest by their very existence – a well-preserved ring of walls enclosing the heart of Londonderry City, still accessible to walkers today and providing a ready-made lunchtime circuit, free of traffic, for the most athletic runners from neighbouring schools. The historical and political resonance of these walls is immense, of course.

Other Places

Local residents will want the reader to know of places in Ulster which they favour and which fall short of international recognition. I think at once of Slemish Mountain, that distinctive feature of mid-Antrim where Saint Patrick herded the sheep in his day. (The reader ought to be warned at this point of the habit we have in Ireland of calling every hill a mountain and every village a town.) Or of that elegant spot at Downpatrick Cathedral where Saint Patrick is believed to be buried, and where I heard, as the personal guest of the town clerk, a most moving performance of Handel's Messiah – two hundred years after its first performance in Ireland, its first performance anywhere.

There is a town street in the City of Armagh so long, so wide, so green and so well-turfed that it is universally referred to as 'The Mall', and it lies close to those two cathedrals looking at one another across the rooftops. Some would rank it amongst the great civic beauties of the United Kingdom.

Where else do local people take their visitors in the month of May than to Rowallane in the heart of County Down when they want to show off one of the finest displays of heather, rhododendron and azalea?

If the freshest of air, the breath of the real sea, and the salty taste of the ocean are what your visitor yearns for, then take him to Portrush, built over a rocky promontory at Ramore Head, jutting out into the Atlantic Ocean and washed by the wind and the rain on its eastern, western and northern flanks. These are amongst the things I miss most in England where the sea, by comparison, often seems just second-hand sea.

Drive up a half a mile at Downhill to the modestly prepared viewing point at Eagle Rock, Benone, and look down on a well-drawn map – for that is what it seems to be – and see the whole of Magilligan laid out before you, with every farm, farmhouse, cottage, local school and all else clearly visible. This includes the Presbyterian Meeting House where Stella and I have arranged with the minister to have our ashes buried when we die.

Belfast's own seaside resort – Bangor County Down – although now a designated 'growth town' under the Matthew Plan, includes a little municipal park that is the embodiment of Ulster's desire for cleanliness, neatness and orderliness – the Pickie, overlooking the Pickie Pool and Bangor Bay itself.

On round the North Down Coast – and this confirms the concept of small towns separated only by a few miles – lies the fishing village of Donaghadee where all you had to do in our day was to persuade a fisherman to take you out a mile or two to the Copeland Islands, a group of low-lying uninhabited islands used for the grazing of sheep. No wonder that even our children, normally looking for excitement, would pester us with 'When will you take us to the Copeland Islands again?' so as to be able to tell their friends of their adventures – in terms of their imaginations.

family in Place and Time

Magilligan, a flat peninsula in County Londonderry lying between Lough Foyle and the Atlantic Ocean, was the homeland of my mother, Martha Sherrard (or Shearer in the vernacular). Derrybeg, a few miles away in the fertile orchard country of the River Roe valley was home to my father, Robert John (who was noticeably less enthusiastic about that bare treeless backwater, as he saw it, than the rest of us were).

Both were of solid farming stock, deeply rooted in the Londonderry countryside, who had migrated there from Scotland in the seventeenth century.

Active members of the Presbyterian Church in Ireland – a close sister of the Scottish Presbyterian Church – they all moved easily in the network of ministers and elders of the Kirk. Married in 1904, they soon moved up to the expanding city of Belfast where the best employment was to be found. Times were good and comparatively peaceful.

My parents bequeathed a healthy constitution to each of their seven children (four girls first, then myself and two other boys), a constitution based on the solid virtues of their country lifestyle: hard work, open air, walking everywhere, and a simple diet of butter, milk, cream, buttermilk and eggs (from hens, ducks, geese and turkeys) along with a pronounced addiction to fresh herrings from an itinerant dealer with a cart, who offered them in lots of a dozen at a time.

They were lucky – and we were all lucky – to find good schooling in Belfast, even if the state of school buildings left much to be desired. In my third year at primary school there were eighty of us nine-year-olds occupying one classroom – part of the legacy meanly left to us by the British administration when handing over to us in 1920 – and which we managed to put right all over by 1939. But throughout town and country there was a widespread tradition of good teaching being expected and delivered.

Magilligan played a much larger part in our lives than did Derrybeg, where the family were preoccupied with a flourishing brickyard and a shop in the town. My mother's brothers, Tom and Harry, were worried by the thought of their sister and the hardships she must be going through with her big family in a terrace house without the support they would normally take for granted, namely a farm, a field, a garden and a hen-house. A sack of potatoes would often arrive by train and reveal – when you undid the binder twine – a couple of rabbits and a chicken or two.

The only time when we came near to catastrophe was when Uncle James from Derrybeg, on being given a bedroom lit by an open gas jet without mantle or globe – a 'fish tail', we called it – conscientiously put out the light on going to bed by using his powerful lungs to blow out the light, leaving the gas to go on flowing through the open tap.

More than all that, the frugal farmers allowed themselves the luxury of a visit each year to the three-day show of the Royal Ulster Agricultural Society, arriving unannounced and confident that Martha would put them up comfortably for a night or two.

Far more important than those sporadic events and of much more lasting value was the reception always waiting for us without question on the 300-acre farm at Ballymulholland, Magilligan. Every school holiday one or more of us would travel the sixty miles or so by train – and later by the splendid bus service run by HMS Catherwood – in the full knowledge that no jolly entertainment awaited us, nor relaxing week in a deckchair. As soon as we arrived on the farm – a mile from the main road – Aunt Isobel, the embodiment of big-heartedness in every sense, would push a basket of tea and soda scones into our hands for us to take out to the men working in the outlying fields or with instructions for bringing in the cows for milking. In that and a dozen other ways all seven of us absorbed the essentials of daily life on a mixed farm, the succession of seasons, the sequence from year to year of grain, root crops, lea and so on – and, above all, the procreation of the animals and the poultry – a deepening of our education that was to last for all our lives.

The horizons of our lives were extended by the family contacts we had with the New World. Relatives who had emigrated to Canada or the States kept in touch with their homeland and my father responded by sending out a steady flow of Coleraine and Londonderry newspapers to lessen the pangs of their homesickness. At times events in America would even seem closer in some ways than events, say, in London.

My father was a highly intelligent man, affable and outgoing, well-read and well-travelled within the British Isles. We were proud of him when he struck up a friendship with our schoolteachers, happy to discuss with them the Shakespeare play he had seen at the Grand Opera House each time such popular actor-managers as Charles Doran or Frank Benson appeared on one of their many 'positively final tours' of the provinces. Employed at the linen department of Robinson and Cleaver which, in the years following the end of the war in 1945, built up a good line of business with wealthy customers from the United States, he enjoyed talking with them about affairs in Ireland and Scotland and the novels of Sir Walter Scott, all of which he seemed to have read and remembered. In the process the linen department became a recognized stopping place for Americans, and my father must have become an unacknowledged asset to the firm. (In a way they were following the pattern set by Aunt Jackson at her draper's shop in Limavady, for she not only detained her best customers for a bit of chat but insisted on giving them tea and cakes in a back room.) Father was a liberal in politics, hoping to see a united Ireland within the British Empire of his day, a wishful thinker to the last.

Such salesroom conversations with visiting Americans would naturally turn to the famous beauty spots with which we grew up: the Antrim Coast Road, the Giant's Causeway, the 'Mountains of Mourne that sweep down to the sea' and the well-preserved Walls of Derry. One of the many benefits of living in a small province is the opportunity to see such features not once or twice as the tourist does but several times, in different weathers, in different company, and in different circumstances. I had, for example, often travelled on the Coast Road without taking much heed of the people who lived there. Then, while I was Chairman of the Boys' Clubs, we began to run weekend training courses for club leaders and we quickly came to understand something of the lives of those who lived and worked there when we had to deal with a local farmer or buy our provisions at the village shop.

When, soon after the war, that is to say 1946 or thereabouts, it fell to me to chaperone wealthy Americans to the Giant's Causeway I was amused to hear them nonchalantly demand a separate bathroom attached to each hotel bedroom. I thought it a needless luxury, if not actually sinful extravagance. I reckon that it was some sort of mark of progress when, by 1970 or so, every hotel and boarding house was expected to be offering 'rooms en suite'.

I had, like many others, spent happy days climbing on Slieve Donard, Binyon or Bearnagh without much thought for the wider pattern of that granite mass. The perspective changed for me when Simon was awarded a certificate on his completion of the 'Mourne Walk' – a strenuous trek around the granite wall that marked the limit of the Water Commissioners catchment area in the heart of these uplifting hills – a walk which, when all the ups and downs are reckoned, measures 22 miles in length and 10,000 feet in height.

Our boys grew up enjoying walks in the Ulster countryside using the youth hostels, which remained simple, remote and unserviced. I was one of those on the committee who stoutly resisted any thought of 'walking by motor car' and surviving by the process of buying a made-for-you meal from the warden. An English youth hosteller on his first visit would no doubt look on such conditions as 'backward' until he woke up one morning in a thatched cottage on the shoulders of Benevenagh, let us say, ready for that simple pleasure of boiling a big brown egg given to him the previous evening by the farmer's wife, and toasting one of her soda-farls on the embers of an open turf fire.

It would be no exaggeration to say that, in the course of some seventy years or so spent in and around my homeland, I must have stopped a hundred times to admire the cliffs at Downhill with that extraordinary little temple on the cliff edge, without appreciating much of their potential. Going up one day in 1990 with my friend and colleague Cecil Newman, a man of many talents, in order to get a professional photograph of Magilligan, I learned a lot. Problems of focus, length, depth, lighting, exposure, patience and so on were solved and the picture of Magilligan, with the strand stretching away almost to Donegal, that now adorns the cover of my book, *Aspects of Ulster,* was the result. That is one of the many reasons why I include my essay 'On Magilligan' as a free-standing and self-sufficient appendix to the whole work. I can say that I had more pleasure in writing that essay than I had in producing any of my other short stories or essays.

A Man's Personal Habits

Inconsiderate in the way he persisted in sending favoured customers from the linen department out to our house without a word of warning and blandly assuming that my poor mother, with her seven little ones round her knees, would entertain them and somehow produce a fine meal out of nothing, my father nevertheless redeemed himself on Saturday afternoons. After a five-and-a-half-day week, spent mostly on his feet, he could produce at midday on Saturday a deep reserve of physical and mental energy. Always favouring a Victorian turn of phrase, he would announce that following his dinner and his noble sanctification he would take a bunch of us out on a voyage of exploration and enlightenment, no less.

As the Belfast tramway system was neatly organized on the pattern of the hub and spokes of a wheel, he was able to plan a trip of genuine interest and novelty at the cost of a few penny tram tickets. Starting with us at Castle Junction, the easily recognized hub, he would take us on a tram all the way out to its terminus on the rim of the wheel. There, there was usually an air of comparative peace as the conductor drank his flask of tea and the driver undertook that perilous task of standing in mid-traffic and repeatedly trying to change his overhead trolley from one line to the other with a long, upturned fishing line – a source of new amusement to us. Then, engaging the tram-men in conversation Father would get from them the best way of walking the mile or two of distance round the rim to the next terminus – say Knock to Belmont, Cregagh to Castlereagh, the Falls to the Shankill or whatever. At a stroke this move took us into the borderland of town and country, of built-up area and open farmland. Where a minute earlier we had been travelling in a clattering, electric vehicle, we were now watching the slow movements of cattle and sheep grazing in the fields. Then back to the hub by that second route where Father would again point out some interesting features. He was especially good at identifying for us those old Belfast villages of the local history books, overtaken by the rapidly spreading city – Ballynafeigh, Ballyhackamore or Ballysillan, perhaps.

The confused Belfast image, that might have left us troubled in our minds, of a meaningless jigsaw of bricks and mortar overshadowed by huge shipyard gantries became, under his guidance, a living place. Times became harder in the 1920s and my father took on the task of repairing our shoes. With some off-cuts of good-quality leather bought at a factory, using his own tools and his last, he managed to keep nine of us dry-shod for several years – until the girls began to get other ideas.

His other active pursuit was running a vegetable plot on land sensibly set aside in the Ormean Park by the Belfast Corporation. One of my clearest childhood memories is of him coming back the mile or so from his plot on a summer evening carrying a bucket full of pamphrey and scallions. What energy!

The Human Touch in Public Administration

'I like to go up to Stormont in the forenoon, horse-whip some officials and get back home again in the evening in time to milk the cow.' That was part of the evidence given to a British Royal Commission on the Constitution of the United Kingdom and, despite its unorthodox style, it came as music to our ears. The speaker was a rural councillor from West Tyrone (whom we did not know) and he was in fact supporting one of our main aims, namely to provide a service at the administrative centre that was handy, open and accessible to all who might have business with it; and in that way he was strengthening our case for the practical benefits of regional devolution.

More often than not a local council would prefer

to send a balanced deputation of selected members rather than just one councillor. They knew, and we knew, that the issues at stake could be intricate, involving some right and proper disagreements. They would appreciate the common sense of coming and talking to us, instead of piling up further angry correspondence or bombarding us with insults from afar. Stormont, situated in its own parkland estate just beyond the fringes of the Belfast built-up area, with ample parking space and pleasant meeting rooms, presented to them an attractive prospect which we did little to discourage. Indeed, an old hand whom we had inherited as an Assistant Secretary from the former British administration in Dublin Castle before 1920 used to delight in chiding us by alleging that we received more deputations from our small province in a month than they did from the whole of Ireland in a year. So be it, we said.

The heads of other Ministries had their own ways of keeping in touch with the leading people in their particular fields – farming, schooling, industrial promotion and so on. Having little faith in the practical value of cocktail parties and the like, I had worked out a little scheme which I found both useful and agreeable. Each year, during the summer, I would set aside two or three days, shut up shop (for I knew I was not indispensable) and drive myself to our outer flanges west of the River Bann in order to pay an informal but planned visit to our outlying councils – Magherafelt, Lisnaskea, Irvinestown, Castlederg, Limavady and so on. My object was not to try to settle current problems but to let the Town Clerk (or other chief officer) talk to me about his current worries or even just to encourage him to let off steam. For my part, I liked to refresh my memory of the offices, the staff, the surroundings and the look of the area generally. If the Mayor happened by chance to drop in on us, so much the better.

Anxious to try to convey to readers a sense of the odd mixture of cussedness and genuine friendship in the Ulster character, I recall the days when I was retiring from departmental work and when people were paying the usual tributes and saying nice things. Castlederg RDC, our most outlying council far to the west of County Tyrone and close to the border, spoke warmly, not of anything I had ever done for them officially but of the effort I had made to drive through a snowstorm in order to be with them on the morning after they had suffered some terrorist outrage.

Any government central body exercising its statutory responsibility to give or withhold approvals, consents, grants and loans in a democratic system is bound to attract criticism. We attracted our share or rather less than the share we might have expected, as I look back on my exposed position in senior and central positions. I include the years of my apprenticeship as Private Secretary to several Ministers in whose offices grievances were most likely to be handled. Some were politically motivated, some ill-founded, some trivial in the extreme, but in my estimation not nearly as many substantial grievances as the general political atmosphere would lead anyone to believe. This was due to some extent to the close relationships that I have been mentioning, but to a much larger extent to the high quality of the administration. There is much nonsense talked on the subject and I have no intention of repeating here the account of it all that I gave at length in my autobiography, nor arguing the matter afresh. I content myself with quoting for the convenience of the reader this quotation from that impeccable journal, *The Irish Jurist,* Volume XII pp. 389-92, where Professor W. N. Osborough wrote, 'Were it not for the inherent instability in the order of things and the violence and civil strife that took over in the years after 1968, the achievements of the Northern Ireland Civil Service might well have been written in letters of gold.'

More relevant and even more authoritative are the findings of Sir Edmund Compton, who held at one time the literally unique position of Ombudsman for the United Kingdom (including Northern Ireland of course) and of Ombudsman specially for Northern Ireland. Facing a press conference reported in the *Belfast Telegraph* on 27 January

1971, he said that he had found a high quality of administration in the Stormont government – almost to a fault. An individual here received noticeably higher consideration than those in any other part of the United Kingdom. From the point of view of efficiency it was almost too high; for the citizen it was all to the good. There was not one incident of culpable action by any organ of government. All in all and bearing in mind the many ups and downs of politics, government and administration since 1920, the State could hardly have survived without such a competent, dedicated and impartial civil service.

I committed myself in my autobiography [p.239] to the following one-sentence paragraph: 'I am proud to have belonged to such a Service.' I came to appreciate what a resonant chord I had struck only when private messages of support for that crucial sentence began to reach me from trusted colleagues of all ranks. Following thirty years of retirement I stand by that sentence today.

Back to the Family Farm

Wishing to show readers something of the strong feelings of Ulster people for the land, I now take the present-day example of a professor at The Queen's University, a barrister at the High Court of Justice, or a Permanent Secretary at one of the Ministries at Stormont. It does not matter which, as each is an

Ulsterman at heart and is at the top of his profession. Deciding to go down to the home farm for a couple of days, he drives along one of the motorways for forty minutes or so, shedding the concerns of the city for the consolations of the land. Every Belfast man, it is said, still has the glaur of the country on his heels. As well as that, and at a deeper level, he knows that history is a living force within his being and as he changes lanes in readiness for quitting the motorway at Dungannon he hears himself automatically reciting the popular old ballad:

And the faith that they kept
Still learn to keep
Through good report and ill,
So long as the silvery Foyle runs deep
And Dungannon stands on the hill.

He is heading for his Mullaghmore, his Drumfern, his Slievenaman and cannot get there soon enough. Unable to thole any delay, he leaves his car at the manse and steps lightly over the sheugh to greet his friends in that monstrosity of a modern villa, surrounded by an exaggerated ranch-style fence, all replacing an old farmhouse, thatched and white-washed, in which he was born and brought up and where his people have been tilling the land since 1613. In no time he is helping to feed the pigs, stook the corn sheaves, and collect the duck eggs that these negligent ducks keep laying in odd corners.

As he passes the hi-fi system (that seems to have grown every time he sees it) he glances at the chart which he himself had hung up next to it – his attempt at drawing their family tree. He can claim to have had a fair degree of success in tracing the family back to the early seventeenth century. Those well-known deficiencies in the public records in Ireland are compensated for by the continuing existence of much good historical material in private hands – churches, schools, graveyards, landed estates, linen firms, shipping companies, local militias, paramilitary forces and so on. But that entails much time and travel and means harder work than a session or two in the comfort of the Public Record Office at Balmoral Avenue alongside the microfiche. Still, that hard work is compensated for, in turn, by the inborn informality and lack of stuffiness in meeting the responsible people or in gaining access to key buildings. Hopefully, he says, those valuable assets are not going to be destroyed by the war against terrorism and all the security measures now being recommended. His own administrative experience tells him that the solution can lie only in an intensified drive by the Record Office to persuade more and more holders of private documents to hand them over for safekeeping and controlled access.

On good advice he had settled on 1613 as his starting point, and it is proving to be as good a starting point as any for examining the great movements of Scots to Ulster at different times in the seventeenth century. But his inquiring mind drives him to keep on asking: Who were these Scots? What part of Scotland did they come from? Why did they come? And so on. To pursue these sorts of inquiry back beyond 1600 in Scotland itself would call for much more effort and travel – a job for another day, he decides, as he prepares for bed in the spacious bedroom he is occupying, complete with en-suite bathroom.

Great Engineers of Ulster

My nephew, John Moore, an experienced mechanical engineer of Holywood, County Down, had already supplied the facts needed to bring this chapter towards a fitting conclusion. What better climax to a 'Perspective from Ulster' than an account of the invention of the farm tractor by Harry Ferguson – a household name in Ulster and at the same time a brand name known to the industry far and wide.

Professor Sir Bernard Crossland (Dean of Engineering, Senior Pro-Vice-Chancellor of The Queen's University) and John Moore co-operated in producing a fascinating volume, *The Lives of Great Engineers of Ulster* (Belfast, 2003). Foremost among the twenty-five remarkable engineers who have been responsible for inventions and innovations of top quality and importance is Harry Ferguson, whose picture appears on the cover and whose brilliant invention is classed by the two authors 'as one of the greatest inventions of the twentieth century'. Farming was transformed in every land by the use of the farm tractor developed and improved by Harry in the early years of that century. Farmers everywhere have as a result been enabled to produce more food and at a cheaper rate, and thus enabled to help to feed millions across the globe.

I remember, from direct personal experience, the strenuous efforts being made by all branches of the government of Northern Ireland at Stormont to persuade Harry to build a factory in Ulster (which would have been welcome on many counts), but without success. He was not the easiest man to deal with and he eventually died in 1960 in sad circumstances.

Harland, Wolff, Cameron, Pounder, Andrews and Rebbeck were among the innovators in marine engineering who succeeded in building up the two shipbuilding yards in Belfast (despite the absence of any coal or iron at hand) and who were responsible for a series of ocean-going ships including, alas, the *Titanic* which met her untimely and unhappy fate in collision with an iceberg in the North Atlantic one April night in 1912, as every cinemagoer knows by now.

Away back as early as 1832, another Ulster engineer, Alex Mitchell, had invented the simple but hitherto unseen helical screw piling system which was soon adopted widely for all types of construction in and around harbours, moorings, lighthouses and so on, where complete stability under water is needed.

Another early appearance on the Ulster scene was the Portrush to Giant's Causeway electric railway in 1881, the earliest hydro-electric railway anywhere in the world. It lasted until it had to surrender – most regrettably and needlessly – to the demands of finance in 1949 when, with better support, it could well have remained one of Britain's world-class achievements attracting tourists of every kind to this magical stretch of Atlantic coastline. Is it too late now to revive it in some acceptable and modern form?

Eric Megaw must be recognized as the father of airborne radar in World War II, as he penetrated further than anyone else into the deepest recesses of very-short-wave radio transmission. The leading scientific authorities of the day could find no words strong enough to do justice to this graceful and likeable man's contribution to science and engineering. Eventually they felt forced to speak of his early death, at the age of forty-eight, as '*drenching* for all of us'.

Cyclists everywhere must surely recognize and honour John Dunlop, the veterinary surgeon of

Belfast who, determined to have a more comfortable ride on his bicycle along May Street, invented for himself – and for the whole world – the now familiar pneumatic tyre that bears his name.

Some of the inventions were quickly taken up abroad. The biggest and most immediately practical was Mackie's textile machinery. More unusual, and even more eagerly adopted in the immense tea-trade of India and elsewhere in the East, was Davidson's invention of machinery for the drying of the leaves of tea bushes – a simple system based on the best placing of fans, which took the world by surprise. *The Times* of Ceylon in 1937 went so far as to describe this restless and inquiring man as 'The Man of a Hundred Inventions' – Sir Samuel Davidson of Sirocco fame at a corner of Bridge End in East Belfast, familiar to all of us in the east of the city as we passed by in the tram on our way in and out of town.

I take just one more example of inventiveness from the twenty-five featured in the book, simply because its value to humanity has been measured and proven – the Martin-Baker ejector seat for use in an aircraft emergency. I think of a quiet rural spot in County Antrim where a factory has, since 1957, been successfully producing ejector seats for saving lives on the principles and practice (at once ingenious and highly dangerous to experiment with) developed by James Martin of Crossgar in

County Down. At the time when they were writing, Crossland and Moore reckoned that the invention had saved no fewer than seven thousand human lives.

Let it not be thought that someone like myself is untroubled by doubts and self-examination over his feelings of national identity. Far from it. I, too, had to search my heart again and again in my earlier years and perhaps I can convey something of the conflict of my position in a frontier society in this way. Prolonged research into family history impressed on me the historical depth, the moral strength and the lasting values of my Ulster-Scot ancestry and upbringing. My pulse-rate tells me I am Irish when I see the green jerseys run out on the rugby field at Twickenham, or when I hear the haunting strains of the Londonderry Air, or when I am forced to listen in England to anti-Irish jokes. My reason tells me that I am British in the dimensions of law and liberty. I am proud to acknowledge all three loyalties and I count myself the richer because of them.

On a Death-List

"Your name is on a terrorist death-list, Dr. Oliver, and we are here to offer you this hand-gun for your self-defence". Thus spoke two plain-clothes men from the Royal Ulster Constabulary in my private house one Saturday afternoon at the height of 'The Troubles' in Belfast.

After a lengthy and practical talk we all agreed that, in my situation, perhaps the use of a gun might not after all be such a good idea. I had not been trained in the use of firearms. To be really useful the gun would need to be immediately available at any moment, say in the hallway or the kitchen and not locked away in some upstairs bedroom. My wife and I had five sons ranging in age from twenty-seven down to seventeen, any one of whom might well try one day to use the weapon in some way meant to protect me. I knew enough of these matters to appreciate that "guns breed guns" and that on balance it might not be the wisest course to introduce guns into the peaceful suburb of Belmont. And so, that well-intentioned and generous offer for which I was truly grateful was quickly dropped. The police then recommended other and better measures which we were glad to adopt. I survived that death-threat and have lived to enjoy another thirty years of active, healthy and happy life.

Appendix I

An Unlikely Friendship

It was an unlikely friendship. I do not claim that it was unique or even unusual, but simply that it was unlikely.

Let me say just what I mean in plain words.

The parties were my wife Meta and I from County Londonderry on the one hand and Ruth, a South African Jewess on the other. The place was Tel Aviv, the big brash city growing up on the Mediterranean coast of Israel, right on the actual sea-front. And the time was September and October 1977.

My wife and I can be easily disposed of. We are Ulster-Scot Presbyterians brought up in liberal families but within the stern, some might think bleak, atmosphere of the unadorned Meeting House, Sunday School attendance, early rising, hard work, walking to church or school or friends, accustomed to high thinking and low living, eating up left-overs, saving for a rainy day. We had come on a long-planned pilgrimage to the Holy Land in order to visit the famous Christian Shrines that we had been brought up to revere. We were semi-retired, one could say, in the sense that we still had the old farm at Aughanloo but we had sold our big dairy-herd and gone over to sheep with the result that – for the first time in our lives – we had money in the bank and time on our hands. We were in no hurry, had read some travel books in advance, had come on our own and had set aside a whole month for this great adventure.

Ruth had come to the Promised Land to visit the famous Jewish shrines *she* had been taught to revere. She, too, was on a leisurely and long-planned pilgrimage. When we first spotted her dumpy little figure at Ben Gurion Airport we whispered: a wealthy Johannesburg Jewess, more money than sense, over-dressed, demanding. Then when we found ourselves all at the same hotel – a modest two-star affair – and occupying adjacent rooms, my wife and I naturally did whatever we could to help her settle in. A married couple enjoy so much mutual support when travelling that the least they can do is to be ready to help a woman travelling on her own. Ruth, for her part, being alone was ready for company; conscious of her plump, heavy unattractive appearance she seemed flattered to find anyone at all paying attention to her: and, on top of all that, she was probably intrigued by these well-scrubbed, incredibly naive people from some place near the North Pole.

Ruth needed help or, more exactly, she at once started to agitate with the hotel management in a way that cried out for modest help.

It happened this way. The developers of the hotel, over-anxious to exploit the narrow promontory of land that they had secured overlooking the sea, had insisted on putting up a building of the 'flat-iron' design with a narrow nose jutting over the sea-front and the rest of the building widening out at the back. On the ground floor the nose of the building was naturally occupied by lobbies and reception rooms; on the first floor it was taken up by a big sitting room; and it was only when you reached the second floor that you got a bedroom in that position. Ruth had set her heart on a room with a view directly over the coast and the sea. To us it did not matter one little bit, accustomed as we were to Portrush, the Giant's Causeway, Castlerock and all those wonderful places on the Atlantic Coast where real breakers dash all day and night on the golden beaches; to Ruth from Johannesburg who had never even seen the open sea it was a tremendous attraction. The management were reluctant to move her up that floor as it was otherwise unoccupied and being kept ready for a big party of visitors due to arrive in a few days. Acting as go-betweens we suggested to the Management that Ruth was a special case. To Ruth we pointed out that while the coveted room had indeed splendid views from windows on three sides, it had few other advantages, a wash-basin with hot and cold and nothing else. For toilet and bath she would have to use a general bathroom and share it with anyone else around. As she was absolutely determined, we all gave way and Meta and I helped her to move her belongings up there.

In that way the three of us found ourselves thrown together. In no time we were arranging to have meals together and to make joint outings. The friendship then developed quickly as for example when one evening Ruth was a few minutes late in joining us at table and found that we had ordered something that sounded to her like potatoes and buttermilk! Quickly cancelling our order she told the waiter to bring us blintz, fludden, humus and falafel as a gentle introduction to Jewish cuisine.

One by one the little mysteries that Meta especially had been puzzling over came to be solved. What was a wealthy diamond merchant from Jo'burg doing in the sort of ordinary hotel we had prudently selected for ourselves? Her clothes were not nearly so grand as we had thought at first sight. My wife decided that they were in the fashions of two or three years earlier; and observed that the same garments kept reappearing day after day.

Ruth was talkative, even garrulous, racy and amusing. Her late husband had been a small bookseller, had not been terribly successful, had spent more time discussing books with his customers than selling them and had left her with little. Her son, the apple of her eye, resembled his father all too closely and as well as that was too handsome for his own good. He was making little of the business. But, and this is the turning point of the whole story, Ruth was not only a devout practising Jewess but a fervent supporter of World Jewry, of the national homeland and the solidarity of Jews all over the world. That was her passion, the ideal that sustained her. That was why she had saved up and made the great effort to come all this way. We could see, as we talked and talked with her over the weeks, that she was revealing to us a generous perception of Jewry that was the very reverse of the vulgar, prejudiced perception so common in the world of a wicked conspiracy of deceitful money-making Jews bent on exploiting us all. What she subscribed to was a brotherhood and sisterhood of Jews in every country, mutually understanding, mutually supportive.

How would Ruth take it when we would suggest going to Nazareth or to Bethlehem, worse still to Jerusalem? Surely she would be bound to reject all these Christian shrines? Not a bit. She proved to be tolerant and forbearing as we fought our way together through the crowds in temperatures of up to 100 degrees Fahrenheit. Admittedly the scales began to fall from our own eyes as we contrasted the gross commercialism of the shrines with the innocent Sunday-School images we had been brought up on.

We were repelled by the vulgarity of it all. And so we had every sympathy with Ruth when at Calvary (or what is alleged to be Calvary and The Tomb) we found religious sects quarrelling shabbily over rights of entrance and control and where we were pestered by priests in dirty robes plucking at our sleeves begging for money. She just allowed herself once to mutter to us: 'Well I hope you're proud of your Christian heritage, are you?'

The places on Ruth's list which she took us to and which in our single-minded devotion to the Land of Jesus we would never have thought of visiting, were a huge success: the Wailing Wall, the Knesset and, above all, the Memorial to the Holocaust, immensely impressive and moving. This could only be good for us, Meta thought.

I was then keen to see something about the mediaeval Christian Crusades, not exactly part of the Jesus Story but certainly one of the great romantic stories from our history books. Acre, on a splendid promontory on the coast, gave us a striking image of the enormous task taken on by our Kings and Princes from Western Europe trekking all the way across the continent and the seas in order to wrest the Holy Places from the Infidel; Acre captured and lost again repeatedly over the centuries. But so far as Ruth was concerned, this was all a flop. She had never even heard of the Crusades and could not work up any interest whatever. But no matter.

As our first trip to Jerusalem had been as part of a Tourist Board coach-tour, I was determined that we should go again but this time under our own steam. Part of the reason was that the Guides, although competent, were far too political and I wanted to see Jerusalem again through our own eyes.

Nothing would satisfy me but a trip in a sheerut. So all three of us got into an empty one (thinking we were lucky) and then had to wait until the Arab driver had collected a total of seven passengers before he would agree to move off. He turned out to be a most agreeable fellow, helpfully making some detours to show us things of particular interest. He certainly did not inflict on us the sort of ultra-nationalist Israeli propaganda that the official guides did. Far from it.

The old phrases from the Bible kept coming back to us: 'up to Jerusalem'; right enough it was up all the way from the coast to Jerusalem, Jerusalem the Golden.

Or 'the Wilderness'. There it was, arid, treeless, dusty, a downright ugly landscape and thoroughly uninviting, the Wilderness that we had learned about in Sunday School. But wherever a farm had been established, what a transformation! Olives, vines, tobacco, cotton, lemons. The desert shall rejoice and blossom as the rose. The industry of the Jewish farmers was prodigious. (That evening after dark we felt guilty as we sped past in our comfortable taxi and saw them still working in the fields by the light of their tractor headlamps. We shall have a lot to tell our friends at home when we give our joint lecture in the Minor Hall.)

Meta was good at entertaining our companions in the sheerut with hair-raising tales of remarkably similar black taxis plying illegally on the Falls Road, each carrying a whole family complete with grannies and children as well as a pram and a bicycle. And that terrifying, blood-curdling story of the young wife who had spent too much time shopping in Donegall Place, was afraid of being late home for her husband's tea and had jumped on to a taxi as it was leaving the kerb – only to find herself deposited half way up the Shankill Road – a terrible fate to befall anyone from the Falls.

Relieved that Ruth had accepted our Christian shrines so calmly and suprised to discover how interesting and moving we had found her Jewish shrines, we came on common ground at the Temple Mount itself when we visited the Great Mosque with its wonderful golden dome and blue-green tiling, and enclosing the very rock from which Mohammed is said to have ascended into heaven. This was stretching the minds and susceptibilities of all of us – and how good for us all, Ruth admitted; but I knew she meant well for *us* in particular.

Ruth told us a lot about South Africa and about her home there. In no time she was pressing us to go out and spend a holiday with her. The only trouble was that any description of her house or garden descended quickly into a tirade condemning the blacks. No words were strong enough to convey the full extent of the fecklessness, the uselessness, the unreliability of the black races. When we protested that Ruth and her friends in South Africa depended on those very same blacks for their comfortable life-style, she rounded on us: 'Don't believe all the propaganda you hear. We would fare better without them. We employ black boys about the house and garden really in order to give them jobs. Where would they be without us? They'd be back in the kraal existing on mealies. Just think that over'. When we fought back she would cap each argument with a story on the lines of: 'If I were to give my garden boy a simple pair of ordinary hedge-clippers and order him to trim my hedge, he would be back in 10 minutes with the clippers broken in two blades. That's the black for you!'

When we spoke of the pictures we had so often seen of happy carefree black men and women dancing, jigging, running around singing in the streets, Ruth would burst out: 'Don't be taken in. They would knife you if you as much as turned your back. And their favourite sport is knifing each other. They are not to be trusted for a moment'. She was hard to stop on this subject. 'Make no mistake; the blacks are savages; they have no idea of personal hygiene for instance; after all that dancing and jigging up and down that you admire so much, what do you think they smell like? They stink, they positively stink.' Well read, broad minded and tolerant Ruth might well be on all other subjects; but on the subject of living with black people her mind was closed, firmly shut, locked and double-bolted.

The highlight of our fascinating visit to Israel was probably a two-day visit to a Kibbutz – Kfar Giladi – away up in the most northerly part of the country and over-looked by Lebanon and the Golan Heights. Here Ruth really blossomed and came into her own. Here was something visible and tangible that embodied her idealism: a self-sustaining community of Jews – men and women on an equal footing – from scores of countries across the world, living and working together in total harmony and mutal respect. There was the added spice of danger and constant fear of attack so that everyone in this particular Kibbutz at Kfar Giladi took his or her own turn at defending the camp against raids from the Golan Heights or the Lebanon itself. If Meta or I as much as raised an eyebrow on hearing that one settler came from Roumania or one from Argentina Ruth would angrily quote her eponymous heroine in the Bible and cry out: 'Whither thou goest, I will go; and where thou lodgest, I will lodge; thy people shall be my people and thy God my God'.

Although we had some lingering doubts about the

human values in these Kibbutzim we had to admit that we admired, at any rate, the universality and the all-embracing brotherhood that Ruth stressed so constantly. That was for her the greatest principle involved, in practice as well as in theory. If we even touched on the problems of the backward nations and the need to be realistic about some Jewish peoples in the under-developed world, Ruth would silence us with: 'Have we not all one father? Hath not one God created us?'

And so we got back to Tel Aviv from Kfar Giladi glowing with sun, good food and the vision of a new world order. It was the eve of Sukkot and the hotel staff were all busy building little tabernacles and equipping them with symbolic foods. As there was no one free to carry Ruth's bags and as the lift had of course been disconnected for the religious holiday, we threw our belongings into our room and carried Ruth's hold-all – now heavy with souvenirs – all the way up to the second floor for her.

Pandemonium. Movement, laughter, noise, music and dancing everywhere.

People running in and out of rooms. Clearly the expected party had arrived and were settling themselves in: the skull cap, the Star of David, the black hat, the dreadlocks – were everywhere. One group were playing a sort of ring-a-ring-a-roses on the landing. There were a lot of women in the utility room where Ruth had left her ironing; and in the bathroom – Ruth's bathroom, next to her bedroom – half a dozen naked young men were throwing bars of soap around and playfully slapping one another with wet towels.

I recognised the people from descriptions I had read in the travel books at home: happy, easy-going, carefree people who were always popular visitors to Israel.

They were Jews from Ethiopia. And they were black.

Appendix II

Balkan Wedding

August 1983

After long delay and much frustration Myles and Elen finally received official permission from the Bulgarian authorities to get married. With Elen's parents they fixed the day: Saturday 20th August 1983.

Myles asked Simon to be his Best Man and so Simon and Lol had to make the long, tedious, hot and expensive journey from Ajaccio. The rendez-vous fixed with Myles was a railway junction somewhere in the Serbo-Croatian mountains, as Myles was travelling by train from Munich. This all worked. Quintin travelled from Glasgow by air on Monday 15th to Sofia where Myles and Elen picked him up and took him by car to Plovdiv, Elen's home, 150 km away.

Stella and I had arranged a modified package tour with Balkan Holidays Ltd in London. This let us fly direct on 13th August from Manchester to Varna on the Black Sea, have a few days there, then by our own devices to Plovdiv for a week before and after the wedding itself, back to Varna to recuperate and so home again by an easy direct flight to Manchester on 27th August. Thus we had the bare essentials fixed in advance but with total freedom in every other way.

We decided not to inflict a day-by-day diary on our friends as we did last year but confine ourselves to the high-lights.

The Varna branch of the family

On our first full day in Varna – quite a stylish sea-port and naval town – we decided to call on Aunt Sofka who lives in a nice old house in a tree-lined avenue in the town centre. Our idea was to present ourselves at Noon on the Sunday, pay a courtesy call and come away. But Aunt Sofka turned out to be a most capable and resourceful woman. Sizing up the situation in a moment she pressed us to stay for lunch. She and her husband Ivan were expecting three young Germans from the DDR – Sven, Karin and Babette – so Sofka and Ivan quickly re-arranged a table set for 5 to accommodate 7. The Germans turned out to be extremely nice, most courteous and proper – a lesson to us all. First we had a cold soup of yoghurt, cucumber, dill and walnuts; then some baked fish; salad; moussaka; and a huge bowl of fresh fruit. Sofka, a retired schoolmistress who had taught German (and other subjects through German) in a special German school in Varna, has immense presence and poise. For example when she came to hand over little, carefully prepared gifts for her invited guests we were ready to be left out, naturally; but with great presence of mind and sang-froid she produced a gift which included Stella and me both.

Sofka is a cousin of Elen's father Nickolai. Ivan is the economics editor of the local newspaper. Son Peter (Elen's cousin) and his wife Vanja live in the small apartment with them. He is a graduate engineer and she a doctor. We met them later. A most enjoyable lunch-party and a quite remarkable performance by Sofka as hostess. But Myles had advised us to that effect in advance. Bulgaria at its most agreeable.

Erasto

That evening as we were struggling to order a meal in a popular restaurant – a most difficult undertaking – a young black boy at the same table offered to help – Erasto Mapaba from Tanzania, now a medical student in Varna. He had applied for a place in any English medical school but had been rebuffed: no places available, try again next year. Hard on the heels of that refusal came an offer from Bulgaria where he is now half way through his 6½ year course, studying medicine through the medium of the Bulgarian language, hoping eventually to become a surgeon and to go back home. Not as dejected as the black student we had talked to in Plovdiv last year, nevertheless Erasto was dispirited, little to do, drifting around cafes – a victim of political circumstances. He is to visit a friend in Blackburn soon and so we asked him to come and stay with us for a night or two in the Lake District.

Church

Attracted by the look of a Greek Orthodox Church we went in and attended a service on the Saturday evening – old, dusty, not well kept but of course heavily decorated over every inch of wall and ceiling. Communion consisted of a huge loaf of bread which was passed round and from which worshippers broke off and ate a piece – some even wrapping up a chunk to take home with them. We were struck by the severity of the Priest, tossing the censer regardless of who was in the way and ordering an old lady to her feet as he passed, despite her crippled leg.

Hydrofoil

Although our idea had been to take the train direct from Varna up to Plovdiv for the wedding (400 km), Elen had the bright idea of putting us on a Hydrofoil instead, and phoned through to persuade us. (She is full of bright ideas). Sounded simple: Hydrofoil (called the Kometa) from Varna along the coast to Burgas and then train on the direct line from Burgas to Plovdiv. But what a hassle! No one at our hotel – one of the biggest and best on the Black Sea coast – could help. There are lots of girls at the Reception Desks, all very agreeable and mostly speaking English, French or German. But language is not the problem. It is comprehension. Try as I would I could not convey to them what we wanted to do. Disregard all Tourist Board advice that the Hotels will help you. They just can't understand – even though I use the technique of a little notebook with tear-out pages on which I write down in large clear letters our requirements, drawing little maps as well. One girl eventually turned up an old dog-eared Kometa time-table which proved to be wrong in every particular – times; length of journey; fare. So I set off on foot to find the passenger-boat terminal and experienced the same problems all over again. At one booth – clearly labelled with the international sign for tourist information: "I" – the girl smiled sweetly and kept saying: "Change – No information". Finally I bought our tickets for next morning's Hydrofoil and then had all the same problems over again trying to find out where the Hydrofoil berthed in Burgas, where the railway station was there, whether we could walk with all our bags, whether we could buy rail tickets in Varna – all to no avail whatever. I just could not find one official in Varna who grasped the idea of the Hydrofoil to Burgas and then train (on the main line) to Plovdiv. Not one.

But we kept at it. Next morning on our way in to breakfast at about 7.45 I asked the girl at Reception whether she could order a taxi for us. I handed her a tear-off page with "TAXI 8.45" written on it, with our name and room number. Need I say that when we came down at 8.45, after breakfast and after packing, we found an angry taxi-driver waiting for us for about an hour and just about to drive away in understandable disgust. When he got us to the Boat Terminal there were twelve Hydrofoils in service and no indication whatever of the one we were to sail on nor of the berth we were to go from – he decently tried five and then wisely abandoned us, with our five bags.

All this is a terrible shame, for the Hydrofoil is wonderful and could be one of their show-pieces if they handled it sensibly. The Burgas part worked out all right. The railway station (a period-piece of Anna Karenina style) is just about within walking distance and there was a good train going at 4 in the afternoon, which suited us fine. But the left-luggage office was a scene of utter squalor – two lazy indifferent girls sitting smoking at a wreck of a table, over a half-eaten pudding of some sort, amid total chaos. Good journey, eventually, (and very cheap) to Plovdiv where Nickolai, Dora, Aunt Dora and little Velislav were all waiting for us. I recount these harrowing experiences as a warning to anyone who wants to undertake a bit of independent travel in Bulgaria. You can do it but be warned.

We had a further problem when actually embarking on the Hydrofoil. There were about fifty of us boarding a vessel able to take, say, a hundred. But there was no system. We were all surging to get on to a narrow, rickety gangway where an official was vainly trying to check the names of a large party of people against a list in his hand. Turmoil. When our turn came (with five bags), he rejected our tickets saying that we had paid only 5.50 whereas the proper fare was 7.50. The girl in the Hotel had said 5. The girl at the harbour had charged us 5.50. We were entitled to travel only as far as Nessebur – three-quarter way along, but which we had never mentioned nor even thought of. I insisted on getting on board and promised to talk to the Captain on the voyage. True enough he called me down to his cabin, showing me his official tariff which showed quite clearly what the proper times, journeys and fares were. I insisted that we had done nothing wrong but had been wrongly served by the harbour office. He saw the point. As he had no supplementary tickets nor even receipt forms, he gave in and said he would take us the whole way. When I told him about the wedding he melted entirely; we shook hands and parted the best of friends.

Open Currency Voucher

When we were ordering our main travel arrangements with Balkan Holidays in London, they charged us an extra £100 for the Open Currency Voucher which they supply. This is a convertible voucher which, they allege, can be quickly cashed and is a great convenience. It is no such thing. It is simply a device for forcing you to spend at least £100 in hard currency. When I presented our voucher at the official, approved, Balkan Tourist desk in our hotel, the girl was aghast, gave up eventually and handed over to a superior. She took fully five minutes to read the two lines of typescript, vowed she had never seen or heard of an Open Currency Voucher before and would have to consult still higher authority. This took ages and produced no result. She then asked us to go and sit down while she consulted still higher people (Sofia, no doubt). After a long time she came over to us, with the cash in Bulgarian levs less 10% for conversion, complete with a docket made out to that effect. We were very cross at all this bother and at the loss of £10 but what could we do? We might have spent days negotiating and got nowhere. The sequel was even more worrying. When finally leaving Varna Airport for home we had to hand in any surplus Bulgarian cash and (what is more troublesome) account for all the money we had exchanged. When I produced the receipt docket for the ill-fated Open Currency Voucher, the official was totally baffled, alleged she had never heard of such an arrangement and asked me to stand aside while she dealt with the scores of ordinary passengers in the queue. Time was passing. Our Flight Departure was imminent. Stella had meantime checked in at the departure desk, sent on our baggage to which "Hold Back" notices were attached, and been forced to hand in her Passport at the Control Desk. Time was rushing by. Finally I pressed my official to accept the dreaded docket and let me go on, which she did. As I joined Stella at the Control Desk and had my Passport checked, we asked for Stella's, only to hear the Passport controller deny that he had it! He was not the same man!! The previous one who took her Passport had been relieved by a fresh colleague who did not know what we were talking about. When I explained that we had been separated, he replied: "So you are divorced, are you?" Near panic, for a moment, but all was well in the end.

I am writing to Balkan Holidays Ltd about this whole business rejecting the arrangement for these Vouchers and asking for my ten pounds to be returned. Believe it or not, a handsome apology and a cheque for £10 drawn on the People's Bank of Moscow arrived here on 16 September!

Meal Vouchers

They also have a system of meal vouchers which is written up in glowing terms in the literature but which can be tiresome too. Sometimes it works and you can use them for a meal in any Balkan Tourist Restaurant; but they are sometimes rejected – quite arbitrarily – and it is impossible in practice to argue the issue with a harassed waitress in some crowded restaurant late in the evening.

Aunt Sofka again

Sofka does everything with style – old-world style perhaps, the best old German style certainly – but with style nevertheless. One day we found a beautifully written card waiting for us, inviting us round for 5 o'clock tea. This was a little gem. She was alone this time and sat us down at once to table, handsomely set with a crochet cloth and elegant crockery. She was determined to let us have true Bulgarian delicacies: first, some cheese filo pastry perfectly served; then what we call "french toast" (bread fried in egg mixture) served with honey or apricot jam, or yellow cheese or white (sheep's) cheese; then apple cake; a wonderful cream of sour milk, lemon juice, chocolate-flavoured vanilla pudding and a fresh fig; and finally black grapes. Each was produced as a separate little surprise treat. Ivan joined us later, muttering modestly that he did not normally get such delicacies for his tea; he is a quiet man, with a humorous expression, who managed to convey a lot about Bulgarian economic and social affairs, with wisdom and tact. Sofka all the time keeps going on, a senior academic accustomed to handling people and speaking a rotund German with carefully articulated clauses and sub-clauses. Each time I committed myself to a complex sentence she showed every interest, agreed with what I said and very nicely repeated my sentence – with the syntax improved! The tea session lasted till 8 pm when Sofka organised us all for a walk in the Marine Park – a long, extended affair stretching for 2 or 3 km alongside and 20 m above the Black Sea coast – charming, well-kept, lots of flowers, no litter, no vandalism, no unruly or unseemly behaviour. She showed us the Youth Theatre tucked away in a corner and the Open Air Concert arena. When we commented on the complete absence of flies or midges under the lamps on a warm summer evening she explained that the Town Council spray a given area every single day and announce in the Press in advance which areas are to be done so that bee-keepers and others can look out. They do some things very well and the Varna front is one of them.

A gem of an afternoon and evening.

Week running up to the wedding

Before we describe the wedding day we must recount what happened in the preceding week.

Simon, Lol, Myles and Quintin – with Simon for once in the position of head of the family – were all happily installed when we arrived. They had started off (as required by Police) at a hotel but found it far too expensive and inconvenient for a whole week; so Nickolai obtained permission from the Police for all of them to stay with Elen's family in their two-bedroom flat. All very chummy but what a squash, with mattresses, clothes, bags, papers all over the place including veranda and kitchen. Stella and I stoutly remained at our hotel – the Leipzig – a modest place with obvious deficiencies but friendly and helpful. In the end we became attached to it and were sorry to leave. But sleeping and breakfasting there was the limit of the independence we managed to achieve. Each day we would announce that we would go off on our own and have lunch in town, only to be told that that was out of the question as Svetlana (a close friend) was to make one of her special Bulgarian lunches that day and we must be there! or that Simon and Lol had offered to do the shopping and make the meal – so we must see what they produced. It was well worth waiting for – a most original and outstandingly attractive meal. All meals are late, by as much as 2 or 3 hours but no one minded. Often when we were at table a friend or a relative would arrive – there were lots of people coming and going all the time – and join us for the meal or for a course. There was absolutely no plan to the proceedings. Naturally there were 101 preparations to make for the wedding and we helped where we could grasp what was going on – which was but seldom. There was no explanation and the Bulgarian mind simply does not run in that direction. We might wish to know some little item. Myles would ask Elen as she whizzed in orbit from one room to another without touching the floor. She might toss some scrap of information to Myles of which he might pass on a fraction to us (with his down-beat humour). We would try to pursue the matter with Aunt Dora (very helpful) but by that time a new batch of friends had arrived and the thread of the story was lost for ever. Another feature was the great crowd of school and college friends and colleagues from work (Alen Mak, the big cosmetics firm) who were always around to be greeted, kissed and so on. Elen knows everybody in Plovdiv and is obviously immensely popular with her contemporaries. Our boys, being of her generation, quickly got on to their wave-length in a way that Stella and I could not do and they saw new dimensions to the whole situation. There were many inquiries about Julian and Marcus and their families and much regret that their work kept them from travelling so far at that time.

Thursday 18th was Aunt Dora's big occasion and she has certainly a sense of occasion. She asked us all in for tea at her house (just next door) – Myles, Elen and her mother Dora; Simon and Lol; Quintin; Svetlana, Stella and me as well as Tessie the

Bridesmaid. Tea was beautifully prepared, with gilt china set out carefully on a low table, tea and coffee, two kinds of cake followed by a formal cake with icing. Her little grandson Velislav (aged 5) appeared, made a bow and said: "Good afternoon. I am glad to see you", grabbed the toys we had brought and raced off to his Apache friends in the street. Stella and I decided to use this, the only occasion we could discern that had any pattern or shape to it, to hand over some presents. For Aunt Dora who was to act as official interpreter at the wedding Myles had asked us to get him a book – an illustrated volume on the children of our Royal Family! This went down wonderfully well. We conveyed to Myles and Elen some practical gifts from our neighbours, the Drivers; cards from Uncle Harry and a letter from Julian and Clare; Quintin who had brought a heap of goodies with him produced some Scottish treats for Aunt Dora. We then gave Elen two personal things – a hair slide made of Kendal horn and a string of turquoise beads which Stella had inherited and which must be about 120 years old. Our point in relating this is simply to describe how Elen showed her girlish charm by putting both gee-gaws on at once and twirling round in front of us all. We were greatly touched. Aunt Dora purred with happiness at the evident success of her event and told me privately that it had been for her one of the happiest days in the otherwise drab life she now lives.

Ten Bottles of Whisky

One day Nickolai came over to me in the crowded sitting-room and said, without any introduction or beating about the bush: "I want you to get me ten bottles of whisky". Dumbfounded (I had never seen ten bottles at one time, to say nothing of buying so many) I asked whether vodka or slivova or mastika or some other local brew would not do just as well. No, he replied, it must be best English whisky and nothing less than ten would do. He meant Scotch, of course. Simon quickly straightened me out and together we went round to the Corecom (the shop where you can buy anything for hard, foreign currency). For sixty dollars we selected the most picturesque and memorable bottles: 3 of Johnny Walker, three of Teachers, three of Black and White and (to make up the ten) one of Vat 69 (bringing off that threadbare old Belfast joke that Vat 69 was in fact the Pope's telephone number. This joke went down surprisingly well, as we heard it repeated in Plovdiv for days afterwards). As Simon said to me on the way back: "This is the real baksheesh; every official has to be rewarded for services rendered, or to be rendered".

The family scene again

Benign chaos reigned; but as Simon rightly pointed out everyone remained good-humoured and we never heard a cross or snappy word.

Dinner Party

One evening our boys decided to give a special dinner party for Nickolai's sixtieth birthday and for the fortieth anniversary of our marriage. They took us to a remarkable restaurant in the Old Town of Plovdiv which consisted entirely, it seemed, of balcony rooms opening out into the open air. Everything was late, service was slow, the food indifferent but it was nevertheless an enjoyable and memorable evening. When we arrived we found one big table prepared for us, with four huge bowls of black grapes set out – just as it would have been a thousand or two thousand years ago – or maybe three thousand. It gradually became clear to us that the Bulgarians had come for the company, the music and a night out rather than for the food.

Change?

We were approached many, many times in the street by touts wanting to change Bulgarian money into desirable Pounds or Dollars and offering favourable black-market rates. I was mentioning this to our boys when Quintin capped my story by describing how once when he was swimming in the Black Sea a fellow had swum alongside him, hissing "Change?" But even that story was capped by Myles who described how when he was nervously ski-ing in the Rhodope Mountains last Winter another ski-er swooped alongside him on his downhill slalom and hissed into his ear: "Change?"

Swatowe

We are most fortunate to have Nickolai and Dora
Hadjiilieva as co-parents-in-law, or (as they say)
as Swatowe. Bulgarian, like Russian, has a precise
word for each of all the family relationships – far
beyond any of the Western languages. Nick and
Dora are intelligent, hard working, modest people
and extremely likeable. Both have responsible
positions – he as an chemical engineer and she as an
organiser at the big Plovdiv International Exhibition.
Nick is now retiring at 60 but Dora has a few more
years to go. We like them both immensely. The
word running round the wedding people was that
Elen has inherited her father's intelligence and her
mother's wisdom!

Weather

It was cool and wet when we first arrived in Varna
but the weather then took up and was delightful for
all the rest of our stay – sunny and warm but not
too hot – say 75° to 80°F, with a bit of cloud and
some breeze. We had been told that August '82 had
been unbearably hot so we were all in luck.

Evening before the wedding

Preparations came to a climax on the Friday
evening when the family had a big exchange of
wedding gifts. Myles and Elen had received a lot
of lovely gifts from local friends and these were

heaped up on the table and sofa. (We had advised our friends in the West not to try to send things to Bulgaria because of the postal and customs difficulties and because of the added burden of transport on Myles and Elen. We can all see what they need, later on when they are installed in their new home). The high-light of the evening was the gift from Myles to Elen of a ring with a tourmaline stone exactly matching her eyes. There was also of course on view the famous wedding dress which Myles had chosen and bought in Munich. Simon and Lol gave and received handsome gifts. Stella got an embroidered blouse and a pair of gloves; I got a wonderful Bulgarian jacket knitted by hand by Svetlana – a labour of love if ever I saw one – and a shirt. It turns out that Bulgaria makes the best shirts in the Eastern bloc! We had obviously blundered by releasing our gifts on the earlier day at Aunt Dora's but no regrets; it spread the activity and interest out a bit and involved Aunt Dora suitably.

The Wedding Day – Saturday 20th August 1983

As the final documents of approval were not received until Thursday 18th, Dora and Elen had understandably and prudently held back from inviting the wider circle of friends until then. This left just two days and meant phoning round madly to everyone. Elen was never off the phone and as the instrument was on a wall in a lobby directly between the over-used kitchen and the over-filled sitting-dining room, all of us had to push past her as she went yak-ety-yak all day long. But it is results that count. Everyone sympathised and understood with the exception of just one man who was sniffy about the short notice; in all 110 guests turned up.

We had gathered from someone that it is an essential folk custom for the women of the extended family to collect at the house in order to help prepare the bride, for an hour or two; so we arranged with Simon, Myles and Quintin to get out of their way and come over to our hotel for breakfast. This turned out to be a most happy occasion, in a beautiful breakfast room with masses of flowers and plants (often photographed for their national tourist literature). As we had by then mastered the difficult art of ordering we managed a pleasant and ample meal at the end of which we could not help noticing three typical attitudes: Simon still wincing at one of Dad's weaker jokes; Myles stretching out an arm (five feet long, I'll swear), swiping a hunk of uneaten cheese from Quintin's plate, covering it with a thick layer of sticky red jam and scoffing the lot; Quintin announcing, quietly but firmly, that he would be needing the bathroom to himself for twenty minutes.

Stella, Quintin and I took a taxi and got to the House of Weddings by about 10.40 in the vague belief that something would happen around 11. This is a fine big house in the beautifully restored Old Town, with handsome reception rooms opening off one another. We had the chance of seeing earlier wedding parties come and go and watching the folk customs – no confetti or rice thrown but a big loaf of bread broken open and everyone invited to nibble a piece. We were greatly helped by the Bridesmaid's mother who explained things to us and by Mishka an elderly colleague of Elen's who is in addition – of all things – a Presbyterian Minister preaching to a congregation of 80 to 100 local worshippers every Sunday morning! Speaking fluent English – he had been educated in America – he re-assured us as the hour passed 11 o'clock with no sign of the bridal party: "All Bulgarians are late for all appointments". By this time Simon and Myles had made a most dramatic entrance. The two dogs had sussed out the area on the previous day and had spotted a grand, curved, stone staircase directly opposite the House of Weddings. So they had ensconced themselves at the top and out of sight until 10.55 and then came strolling down this magnificant stairway as in the opening scene of some Fellini film. Most cinematic: Myles in an elegant, cream-coloured Italian suit and Simon in a white suit with a thin chocolate stripe that gave a pink effect overall. But, horror of horrors, the Bride and her parents and all those women folk at home were in a panic because custom requires the Bridegroom and Best Man to be there, apparently, and to travel with them: Not a hint of that arrangement had been given to Myles or to any of us. Mercifully one of Elen's friends (Rumy) spotted the crisis and phoned home to explain. In a trice the Bridal Party arrived all smiles, not in the least embarrassed; no one noticed (as Mishka had forecast); and the ceremony began.

First in a small upstairs room the Bride and Groom, Best Man and Bridesmaid were seated before a splendid formal table and we, the parents were standing behind them. A Lady Registrar fussed over the documents, assisted by two slinky acolytes, with Big Brother looking down on us all from the wall. We were horrified when Nick and Dora kept on chatting and asking questions of the Registrar; and still more horrified when the Registrar hurriedly sent a young man out to buy a bottle of champagne! But these were only the preliminaries, deliberately gone through in order to make certain that everything was in order. Finally, two rings were placed in a casket and off we went in procession led by Velislav as Page in a frilly white shirt and black velvet breeches and by a little Flower-girl aged three, a real dazzler. Through the waiting guests in an ante-room, all bowing to the Bride, and on into the Marriage Room itself to the sound of Mendelssohn played with glorious trumpet-sounds. The crowd then followed us through.

Here the real Registrar awaited us on dais, an

elegant lady who conducted the proceedings impeccably. She spoke clearly and well and one could not find fault with anything she said. The whole tenor of the proceedings suggested much more of a family affair than do our weddings. The four parents, for example, were on the dais with the young people. At one point the Bride was instructed to come over and present herself to Stella and me as our new daughter; Myles to present himself to Nick and Dora as their son. Acting as interpreter Aunt Dora translated everything sentence by sentence. The only point at which she was not needed was when the Registrar put the crucial question to Myles in Bulgarian and without waiting for any translation he spoke out loud and clear: Da (yes). The couple then exchanged rings – Elen's bearing the inscription on the inside: Myles 20/8/83 and Myles's bearing her name. Champagne formed part of the actual ceremony, Bride and Groom each quaffing a glass at which the crowd burst out clapping and buzzing with acclaim. Very involving.

Next the eight of us took up our positions at the front of the dais and all the friends and relatives filed past, introducing themselves, shaking hands, kissing cheeks twice over, offering little bowls of grain or of sweetmeats. The whole ceremony seemed to us to place much more emphasis on the parents and family than we had expected and we must say we were well satisfied, for our part. There was much photographing going on – Simon, Quintin, Dilly and Cousin Nick. So many men are called Nickolai that they have to be given a distinguishing nick-name – this was a tall chap and was known as Long Nick. He was terribly English-looking and wore flannels and (we thought) a Methody (Belfast) blazer. We repeatedly reminded all these people of Auntie Betty's request for two good large photos for her valuable album of family weddings.

The reception took place at the Novhotel, a very grand affair built by the French. When we were all assembled (fully an hour had passed) Stella was asked to break the ritual loaf of bread and then Elen and Myles had to walk over a sheet covered with flowers, rose buds and various small items of ritual significance including a pail of water which Elen had to knock over. Lunch was in a huge dining-room, with tables for four, six or eight. The family had chosen the menu with great care and had themselves brought along the cakes.

Simon opened the proceedings right away with a resounding toast and then Myles gave the main speech of the day, a tremendous affair developing philosophical profundities and laced with quotations from the major European writers – an effort that stunned the audience and became the talk of the town. There was no need to create any atmosphere – the folk customs carried the whole thing along. From time to time, for example, a group at one table would cry out: "The wine is bitter!" at which Myles had to take his Bride over to them and kiss her – to sweeten their wine, presumably. Music took the form (surprising to us) of incessant, loud Western rock, and other popular Western songs. This decadent stuff was apparently what this crowd wanted. Across the corridor a humbler down-market party had folk-music and other local tunes. To start the dancing Simon led off with the Bride, looking like a fairy princess in her white wedding dress with see-through arms and shoulders, lace flounces and pink roses. Myles followed with the Bridesmaid and soon we were all on the floor. I was sitting next to a distinguished relative from Sophia (Ludmila). Stella settled down unashamedly to a good old natter and gossip with Aunt Dora. There were grannies and aunties and cousins everywhere. Lol was a wow, looking just as though she had run in from the tennis court with her tousled curls, a slip of a short simple white dress, and a pair of old boot-laces hanging round her ankles – but immensely sophisticated and outrageously French and feminine. All heads were turned. The reception, to our way of thinking, hardly needed the big hotel. One could picture the whole affair taking place at least as well in some remote village – nothing would have been lost and much gained. But it became clear to us that the whole family connection now consists of townspeople and there did not seem to be any true country people anywhere around.

A dozen or so of the family came back to the house afterwards including Bride and Groom who changed out of their formal clothes and merged back into the family once more. Myles amused the company hugely by reading out half-a-dozen quotations he had culled from Pravda that sent them into fits of laughter. We left about nine, with the rest still going strong smoking Quintin's cigars.

Elen was in tremendous form and full of fun. Instead for example of saying to me "I am now your daughter" she would ask, in a mocking tone, "Shall I bring you a nice cup of tea, Dad?" The rumour had it that the wedding, all in all, had cost Nickolai the equivalent of ten months' salary.

Sunday 21st

Elen cajoled her father into letting her take the family car (a most reliable little Iada) and drive us, along with Myles, all the way to Varna where they were having a few days' honeymoon. We were worried by the distance (400 km) and by the fatigue which must surely be setting in for Elen after such a hectic time. But she persisted. The Varna cousins (Sofka, Ivan, Peter and Vanya) were driving back also so we arranged to travel in convoy which turned out to be good fun (an Uncle George arrangement, as we call it). We were pledged to leave at 10 a.m. but what with cups of tea and a delicious lunch we got away at 12.40. Dora is unbelievably hospitable and capable. Elen drove magnificently. The only hitch was caused by me because I forgot to retrieve our passports from the KGB or whoever was studying them and had to turn back (after five minutes) and ask for them. Elen's driving has improved greatly, fast, careful, safe – she is a most able versatile girl. The trip gave us another chance of seeing the countryside which we have now got to know quite well – maize, tobacco, rice, tomatoes, peppers, apples, roses galore and sunflowers by the square mile; donkey-carts, geese; but the abiding memory is of a lonely shepherd herding a flock of sheep in some big open limitless pasture as he must have been doing for countless centuries past. Every ten or twenty miles there is a drinking fountain at the roadside, generally with a lay-by and a bit of shade. We agreed to stop at one for a drink of cold spring water, a wash, a rinse for any fruit and a general freshener. In the consumer society which the authorities have (wisely or unwisely) allowed to develop the modern Bulgarians are now-a-days well kitted out for travelling, with thermos flasks for cold water, cool-bags and so on. But their food remains basically unattractive and the picnic lunches one noticed around most off-putting. A sandwich for example consists of one slice of crumbly bread, unbuttered, with perched on top a piece of cheese or ham or more likely a fat round sausage that constantly rolled off. In compensation of course they have the lovely fruit – outdoor tomatoes, peaches, pears and black grapes.

The Beach

The Black Sea beaches are what the tourists come for and the country's biggest earner of foreign currency. We spent most of our time in Varna on the City Beach directly below the town. Sand good, water pretty clean, some breakers but the attractions are of course the warmth of the water and the strength of the sun. Beaches are all gated and an entrance fee charged. A few amenities such as sun-shades, changing rooms and life-saving master swimmers every 200 yards but not much else. Our beach was hugely crowded; 50,000 people I reckoned on a stretch of less than a mile or 30 to the yard. This gave us an unparallelled chance of studying the human scene. Do not be frightened by that fierce look that Bulgarian men have! Behind that huge moustache, those flashing black eyes and that thick crop of hair there lurks a sugar-daddy devoted to his children, liable to fondle his baby for a couple of hours on end. Varna Beach has one gimmick and it is a huge success – a helter-skelter with water. In your bathing togs you climb up a simple outdoor staircase on the beach, launch yourself into a sort of open channel or pipe made of translucent blue plastic running with water all the time and come tumbling down helter-skelter until you are tossed out finally into a pool. The demand never slackened. Our Bride came down seven times! It is fun also for those on the beach because they can watch the whole circus and can see what look like little mannikins or pipe-cleaner-men through the blue plastic. A great wheeze.

A lot of Germans from the DDR, some Russians, some Roumanians (unpopular) and some Greeks (most unpopular). If anything went wrong in Varna, people blamed it on the Greeks ('they break all the rules') – the rotten Roumanians and the ghastly Greeks, it seemed. A memorable sight every day at Varna is the string of huge cargo ships lying off shore awaiting their turn to dock, as many as ten or twelve of them at any one time. Previously they used to lie close to the beach but new rules prevent them from coming closer than about 5 km in order to avoid pollution. A great sight.

We took a boat trip one day to a quieter beach at Druzba but we did not get to the really big places: Golden Sands or Sunny Beach.

The Street Scene

In all the towns we visited last year and this year we were struck by the delight which Bulgarians obviously take in strolling slowly up and down the main streets – hundreds of them, possibly thousands. They are not demonstrative or excitable – one might even think apathetic but it is hard to say. There are plenty of shops, well-filled but unattractive (apart from one art and craft shop in each town). Clothes shops are dowdy and super-markets grim; the supply of goods seems highly arbitrary. You are quite likely to be told that what you want is off. Even when we saw exactly what we wanted, some Apple Juice in small bottles, we were firmly told we could not have any. Then when something is rumoured to be "in", a queue forms and the shop is besieged. The street scene is otherwise very pleasant, with flowers and fountains and of course ice-cream stalls every hundred yards. An attractive feature is the small self-contained booth with a tiny front window – a derivative, we thought, of the genuine old dark little shop one still sees in Moscow – selling beads and sun-hats and all sorts of fripperies. The women one sees on the street are smartly dressed and the explanation seems to be that most clothes are still hand-made; everyone knows some little woman round the corner who can do wonders. Children are especially well done for, with lovely little knitted suits. Markets are good but relatively dear because they can offer produce that the shops may not have. There are many more telephone boxes to be seen on the streets now but without telephone directories. We assume that these exist but – like maps, time-tables, public clocks, fare tariffs and so on – they are extremely rare.

Hardly any police in sight. I am sure they are not

far away but they certainly do not dominate the scene as they do in Germany, East and West. When one does spot a policeman he will as often as not be sucking an ice-cream or queuing for bread.

Departures

Simon and Lol are back in Ajaccio after a very long, difficult, expensive and dangerous journey for they were, at the last stage, derailed by a landslide in the Corsican maquis. Quintin stayed with friends in Sofia for a day before catching his plane home. Myles was quickly back in Munich, hard at work preparing five sets of tender documents within two weeks and getting everything ready for his Bride who remains in Bulgaria awaiting the grant of her Passport to travel to join her husband, the Thracian Princess still unfree.

> Stella and John
> Laundry Cottage
> September 1983

Please return this eventually and at your own convenience

On Magilligan

It is not enough just to say that Magilligan is special. In what way is it special? What makes it special?

Geologically a raised beach Magilligan forms a most unusual triangle of land on the north coast of County Londonderry. It is entirely flat. The northern side of the triangle faces out to the Atlantic Ocean and is bounded by a curving strand some seven miles long, a beach of firm sand pounded by the huge breakers coming thundering in from America, the next parish. The western side is totally different, formed by the shore-line of Lough Foyle, a low, quiet foreshore of five miles or so where the tide goes out for half a mile and where, even then, the less salty water remains shallow for another half mile or so. The third side of the triangle, to the east and south, is formed by the northern escarpment of the big basalt plateau that stretches from the Cave Hill at Belfast, to Fair Head in County Antrim, to Benbradagh at Dungiven and then across to the cliffs overlooking Magilligan. And these cliffs in turn culminate in the striking table-top of Benevenagh, a bold, distinctive, right-angled peak dominating the whole of North Derry.

The basic soil of Magilligan, a new red sandstone, is what underlies the unique character of the area; fine, dry sand that sustains high quality grass, flowers and herbs as well as farm crops.

But no trees, no hedges, no shrubs, save for a few sally bushes that have been deliberately planted here and there.

Magilligan has always been isolated. Although

lying half-way between two busy market-towns, Coleraine and Limavady, ten miles either way, it was always hard to reach until about the middle of the nineteenth century when the railway came; and later the bus. Twenty-five miles to Londonderry City – which you can just see at the head of Lough Foyle – and seventy-five miles to Belfast. And across the Lough are County Donegal and the Irish Republic.

But the stark details of that severe little geography lesson convey nothing of the real spirit of Magilligan.

The air is clear. And the song of the skylark away high up in the clear, sweet air is unforgettable. So too is the poignant cry of the peewit – the local variant of the lapwing or plover – the lonely liquid call that you never get close to but which haunts you when you go away and which catches you by the throat the moment you come back. And closer to the rocky cliffs at the Downhill end is the little tern wheeling endlessly and putting out its surprisingly sharp cry. And, all the time, depending on the weather at the moment or the weather that is on the way, the crashing sound of the big, long breakers on the golden Back Strand.

No grass anywhere that I know has the delicate scent of the Magilligan grass, laced as it is with herbs. Long before tourism became popular in Ireland, people used to come from far and near to lodge with local farmers specially for the cure – as advertised

– for the benefit they received from living close to those magical qualities of medicinal herbs in good sweet grassland. The taste, the unmistakable tang, of salty ocean air added to the delicious quality of the scents and smells of this unique area.

To handle the soil, to let the soft, fine yellow sand run through your fingers, is an odd experience in the midst of farming land. Crops grow in millen sand, as they say locally, sand that is so soft and fluid that no one would imagine it could even hold up, let alone nourish, saleable crops of potatoes and oats and hay and swedes. Up until forty years ago or so a full rotation of crops was carried through – roots, cereals, beans, peas, hay and even for a time that most laborious and troublesome of crops: flax. With an even finer distinction being drawn between the slightly lower and darker parts of any one field, where potatoes would go and the higher, lighter parts of that field (not that there was much difference in reality, I always argued) where turnips would be sown. Or oats (corn as it is simply called) in the lower parts and rye (for the whiskey trade) in the higher sections. For a time after World War II carrots were thought to be worth trying in this sandy soil but the dreaded carrot-fly did too much damage. To-day it would be fairer to describe the farming more as "ranching" with cattle and sheep taking the benefit of the splendid grass.

Where farm cultivation peters out close to the sea-shore and gives way to sand-dunes this extraordinary soil still produces its own crop of dainty little dog-roses and sharp-sweet, wild strawberries in the rabbit warren. And on the sea-shore itself another crop of sea-weed, cockles, mussels and razor-shell-fish. And miles and miles of marram grass.

To the eye Magilligan has a special appeal springing from the vivid contrast between the flat, treeless plain, the black basalt cliffs and the soft rounded hills of Inishowen in County Donegal. And, all over, the sky, the great big open sky, reflecting the changing moods of the two seas beneath.

Drainage is surprisingly good for such a flat plain. For one thing the light sandy soil takes up the ample rainfall. But as well as that a series of small parallel streams – known locally as Drains, Margymonaghan Drain, Ballymagoland Drain and so on – run down from the escarpment to the sea. Much depends on the good behaviour of the central stream, the Big Drain, which in the old days used to clog and back up. I remember being taken as a child of ten or so by my grandfather Henry Sherrard of Ballymulholland to the Court House in Coleraine where, I suppose now, a Public Inquiry must have been going on into the improvement of the Big Drain and the better drainage needed all around. It seems to have worked.

Although never part of the carefully controlled Plantation of Londonderry by the London Companies under King James I – it remained "Bishop's Land" in the language of the time – Magilligan nevertheless reflects in its people the general make-up of the population of the County, The Ulster-Scots have always been the strongest element: McCracken, Morrison, Linton, Conn, Allison, Shearer or Sherrard, and so on. McLaughlin, McDermott, Quigley, McDaid, Deeny, McCorriston represented the Irish stock. At Bellarena the Heygates and at Downhill the Hervey Bruces, the two titled land-owners, took the lead with their immediate households and servants in the tiny Anglican community on the English model, even to those pathetic tablets on the walls of the nave, recalling young subalterns killed in far-away wars, pointless and irrelevant wars they seem now, looking down across empty pews in a beautiful but forlorn parish church.

But times have changed. The familiar pattern of farmer and farm labourer has been broken and Magilligan now has its full quota of doctors, lawyers, nurses, teachers and traders sensibly choosing to live in its healthy atmosphere and settled community. In a sense it is now commuter-land, providing enviable living conditions for academics at the University of Ulster in Coleraine or professional staff at the many other public boards, hospitals, schools and so on all over the northern parts of the County.

It is a peaceful area. Crime is negligible. It is hard to recall a serious disturbance apart from the occasional smuggling episode to or from the Irish Republic when prices or taxes made that a worthwhile pastime. Everyone is aware of everyone else's loyalties, of what foot he digs with, of where he went to school; but it makes little difference in practice to the daily life. The outward signs are of considerable affluence. People, left alone, go on working, travelling, buying their petrol, selling their goods and services. There is little sport, little shooting or hunting, little evident recreation. People, I suppose, have their own satisfactions. Family connections are powerful. The respect for education is immense. People go to unbelievable lengths to get their children to the big schools in Coleraine, Limavady or Londonderry and from there on to higher colleges far and wide. They know they are lucky to have such choices open to them.

One of the signs, I always think, of a truly settled community is the way in which it can absorb an intrusion however threatening it may seem. When the British War Office, for example, set up a Camp in Magilligan for summer training and manoeuvres some of us thought that the quiet, peaceful Magilligan that we loved would be ruined for ever. Not at all. By leaving the Army to their own devices on the one hand and on the other trading quietly with the commissariat in butter, milk and eggs the local people came out well. The arrival more recently of a prison threatened to destroy the peace in an even more unhappy way; but once more a necessary intrusion was quietly absorbed.

I have always been intrigued by the lively connection between such a remote, rural and (one might imagine) backward area and the big world of education and employment. Again and again that connection strikes those of us who are in love with the place. You do not need to live for ever in the neighbourhood. You may go away and live far off; you may have a career in aeronautics or accountancy or commerce that takes you far away into the wider world. But you belong to the place nevertheless. You are part of it, still. It is a matter of people as well as place, of spirit as well as soil.

Magilligan is a modest place. It does not waste time telling you about famous people who came from the parish. One was a blind harpist who played before Princes. One was Lord Moran who became Mr. Churchill's Physician. But I enjoy myself tracing other odd connections that I think I can conjure up. When we were small children playing in Ballymulholland we used to set up imaginary houses among the sandhills and prepare imaginary meals. Dinner consisted of raw potato sliced into cold water and of course attracted no takers – except one, John McDaid, a great big labouring man, one of the humblest of a humble tribe. To his eternal credit John McDaid flattered us by eating our "dinners", actually chewing and swallowing the raw potato sliced into cold water. Judge our pleasure and pride to-day, seventy or eighty years on, when BBC Radio Four produces Father John McDaid, leading Jesuit thinker and writer, to give us "Thought For The Day" that – I think I can discern – includes a perceptive word on rural Ulster.

The hold that Magilligan has on me comes not only from the five senses that I have touched on here but from deeper sources as well, sources that are human and spiritual and perhaps even more powerful.

One of the greatest benefits to our whole family living in industrial and commercial Belfast was the direct, ready and highly personal contact we had with the farming life in Magilligan. My Mother's parents wanting to support their daughter in the big city kept an open door for her and her seven children. So also did her brothers Tom and Harry. But supreme among them all was Tom's Inishowen wife, our Aunt Isobel, the very embodiment of generosity, hospitality and totally care-free welcome – one of the most remarkable and memorable women in the huge gallery of our family connection. "You City folk," she would cry as she saw us modestly picking at one small potato on the dinner-table and up-ended the big dish of laughing, splitting, floury Up-to-Dates or Arran Banners on to the table for us to enjoy. She made us work, as well, an experience that taught us a lot about animals, crops, procreation, the sequence of the seasons. The crowded happy, memories of those fruitful days bind us to Magilligan in a way that little else could do.

But there are deeper roots. This North Derry coast is the homeland of Olivers, Sherrards, Morrells and all the other branches of our enormous tribe. I see the traces at every turn, running back to the year 1600 at least.

There are still deeper attachments. While the attractions of the five senses are very real, there is for me an even greater attraction in something else, something that has lasted longer than the farms, the family or even the community. The hold that the land and the people have on me is never so strong as the hold of the open air, the sea-shore, the tide, the lonely estuary. It is here that nature moves my soul more powerfully than anything else. The effect is no longer just physical or psychological or intellectual; it is spiritual. The vast expanse. The solitude. The empty strand. The everlasting mystery of the tide at ebb and flow. The big rain clouds blowing up from the western hills. The ineffable blue of the sky once the rain has washed it clean again. The haunting cry of the sea-birds. Love is heaven and heaven love.

Some small-minded reader will say that I exaggerate. Some unfortunate reader who has never written a full-blooded love-letter or – worse still – has never received one, will allege that in this frank and uninhibited love-letter to Magilligan it is a sad case of John once again going Over The Top, complete with his well-known rose-tinted spectacles.

But there is more to be said.

The other day I turned up a 1966 Survey of Magilligan sent to me by my old friend Joe Frey, whom I had helped to welcome as a refugee from Central Europe to Ulster in the 1930s. Writing from The Queen's University of Belfast where he was head of Extra-Mural Studies he had added a foreword to a symposium of extremely learned articles by the Route Naturalists' Field Club.

Where I happen to mention in passing the growth of some herbs in the Magilligan grass, the Survey speaks of Magilligan as "the medicine garden of Europe". Where I mention the skylark and the peewit, the Survey lists some ninety species of birds with details of their varied habitats "which makes the area unique in Ulster". I forgot to mention butterflies, simply taking for granted the happy sightings of a Painted Lady or a Small Tortoiseshell in the stack-garden; the Survey lists sixteen, by Latin and by popular names. Twenty varieties of moth are recorded in "this most important area". Where I mention, I think, three sea-shells, the Survey finds no fewer than eighty types of gastropod on the Back Strand alone, between Downhill and The Point. Where I recall a couple of wild flowers, the Survey records something like four hundred flowering plants, including Salix Repens (the finest specimen seen anywhere) and a climbing madder plant carrying the Sherrard name.

When I was a small boy, my grandfather and my uncles in Ballymulholland used to impress on me the great importance of putting on both my boots before beginning to lace up either one of them. To lace up one boot before putting on the other was sure to bring misfortune. According now to the Route Naturalists it was no less a person than St. Columb himself – my favourite saint – who laid down that golden rule in the Magilligan or Tamlaghtard where he spent much time founding the monastery at Duncrun and preparing to go to the historic Convention of Drumceatt nearby in the year 575 A.D.

One day, some thirty years ago now, a well-known farmer died, tragically killed by a passing motor-bicycle. He had been jolly, gay, musical, the most musical of his tribe by far. As the huge crowd of mourners stood around his small farmhouse away down near to the lonely Magilligan Point, the voice of the Presbyterian Minister rose in the clear sweet air, saying:

"They told me, Heraclitus, they told me you were dead,
They brought me bitter news to hear and bitter tears to
    shed,
I wept as I remembered how often you and I
Had tired the sun with talking and sent him down the sky.
Still are thy pleasant voices, thy nightingales awake,

For death he taketh all away but them he cannot take".
Even death will not separate us from Magilligan.

On Getting to know the Great Essayist
William Haslett

So you think I have made a careless mistake in mis-spelling the name of this giant of English letters? Just wait a moment.

When, on making good some gaps in my knowledge of English literature, I came to read William Hazlitt, 1778 to 1830, I enjoyed his Essays enormously. First, there were so many of them. Next, they were so varied. Then, they were so easy to read. Above all, they were so spirited: he had such strong views, such likes and dislikes, such hates and loves. Here was a writer after my own heart – and I do not make that claim lightly, as you will see.

At one moment you are deep in literary criticism, as for example in the very first sentence of Hazlitt's Lectures on the Comic Writers: "Man is the only animal that laughs and weeps; for he is the only animal that is struck with the difference between what things are and what they ought to be." The next moment you are at a prize-fight, not just as an impartial onlooker but as a fervent partisan, for boxing was one of Hazlitt's passions; and I am amused to find that his favourite pugilist was a certain Tom Oliver. A few minutes later you are setting off on a journey with Hazlitt: "One of the pleasantest things in the world is going on a journey; but I like to go by myself... I am never less alone than when alone." Exactly how I feel. He is one of the few accomplished writers who let you into the secrets of his skill: "It is not easy to write a familiar style ... there is nothing that requires more precision and, if I may say so, purity of expression." Writing? Yes but that is not all. Hazlitt is a competent painter as well and once again lets you into some of the secrets of that occupation: "There is a pleasure in painting that none but painters know. In writing, you have to contend with the world; in painting, you have only to carry on a friendly strife with nature. You sit down to your task, and are happy."

His further advice on painting tells us much about the man himself. Having failed to reach the heights of success with his painting: "I flung away my pencil in disgust and despair," he tells us. "Otherwise I might have done as well as others, I dare say, but for a desire to do too well." How I sympathize.

It is perhaps in his theatre criticisms that Hazlitt's likes and dislikes begin to show most clearly. His analysis of the dramatic power and skill of the Mrs. Siddons he admired so much is stunning: "She produced the most overpowering effects without the slightest effort, by a look, a word, a gesture. Can I ever forget the slight pause she made, as Lady Macbeth reading the letter: 'When I demanded to know more of them, they made themselves into air' (sic) ... the glance at which you could feel the audience quiver and cower."

When Edmund Kean was hooted from the stage in 1814 by a lot of vulgar hoodlums: "The vulgar in their inmost souls admire nothing but the vulgar; the commonplace nothing but the commonplace; the superficial nothing but the superficial." What a champion to have! How it would sustain a Chancellor of the Exchequer to-day, an Archbishop, an Heir to the Throne to have the warm support and brilliant advocacy of a William Hazlitt.

On a totally different plane of admiration and support are Hazlitt's moving tributes to his own father, a poor Preacher who eked out his meagre income by taking pupils for private tuition. Not only does William present his father as a conscientious scholar and teacher but as a man of "stainless integrity." So much so indeed that William once heard "a shrewd man say he would never send a son of his to my father lest the boy should be so schooled in truth as to be disqualified from getting his living in the world." Knowing something, now, of the restless life William Hazlitt senior led, I am all the more impressed by the devotion touchingly shown by the son, the author, the writer.

For a writer he was, above all else. As R.L.Stevenson declared, some fifty years after Hazlitt's death; "We are mighty fine fellows, but we cannot write like

William Haslett." It is important to grasp that truth before we dig any further.

Let us turn now to Robert Lynd for some closer guidance. In one of his most guileless yet penetrating essays Lynd warns us: "Hazlitt was not born to good fortune ... he was the possessor of a demon that fought against his happiness ... He separated from both the women he married and seems to have quarrelled at some time or other with all his friends." Those comments are fully borne out by several of his talented friends. Coleridge, for example: "he has a jealous, gloomy and an irritable pride." Leigh Hunt thought that "I should have a still greater affection for him if he would let me; but I declare to God I never seem to know whether he is pleased or displeased, cordial or uncordial - indeed his manners are never cordial". Even Lamb, the gentlest of men, thought Hazlitt "to be ... one of the wisest and finest spirits breathing" but was forced to add "in his natural state", warning us of Hazlitt's unnatural state, the darker side. And Robert Lynd tellingly interprets Hazlitt's writings with the explanation: "the sun shines on the past oftener than on the present or future".

The human side of Hazlitt's tortured life shows up in his many passionate love-affairs. He seems to have been perpetually in love with some woman or other. His close friend Peter George Patmore, father of the poet Coventry Patmore, has alleged that he never knew Hazlitt but he was in love. Indeed one of Hazlitt's more passionate outbursts occurs in a letter written to Patmore on 31st May 1822 from Edinburgh where, and while, Hazlitt was pursuing his divorce suit in the Scottish Consistory Courts, then more amenable on those matters apparently than the English Courts. I came upon this letter in a charming volume "The Faber Book of Letters." Here William lets himself go in recounting ungraciously his vigorous, impetuous wooing of the Landlord's daughter, Sarah Walker: "a regular lodging-house decoy ... she has an itch for being slabbered and felt ... letting me enjoy her through her petticoats ... admitting all sorts of indecent liberties ... do not let any one else do so, he said to her, no not now, was her answer, that is [simply] because there was nobody in the house to do it with her ... the bitch wants a stallion and hates a lover ..." Very understandably Sarah found all this too much to take and walked away, which was lucky for me as my delicate sensibilities could scarcely have borne any more of Hazlitt's behaviour. There is much more of the same in Hazlitt's "Liber Amoris".

So, where does this leave William Hazlitt in the end? Christopher Salvesen sums up the man: "The best prose writer of his age ... Unfortunately the master essayist also achieved a reputation as a scoundrel, an adulterer, a drunk; and when death came to him on 18th September 1830 he was friendless, penniless and living in a London slum." Other scholars may have sought to qualify that description of his end and to argue that circumstances were not quite so bad; but a vivid picture remains, in all its essentials, of a brilliant mind imprisoned in an awkward, fractured personality. A thrawn fellow, as we say.

Having steeped myself in Hazlitt's writings I then began to ask where he came from and when: the questions of history and geography which need to be answered in any full appreciation of a great man's achievement.

Anthologists, editors, commentators, one after another record "from Tipperary", "the son of a non-conformist clergyman in Tipperary" and leave it at that, obviously relying on the findings of the editor or commentator who went before them and not wanting to delve too deeply into Irish affairs.

I was not satisfied. Tipperary did not seem to me to be the likeliest origin for a Hazlitt. There have been a few Hazlitts in that county but not many and not significant.

In North Antrim and North Derry Hazlitts abound. They have been around in large numbers for centuries. As you drive along the main road in the Castlerock area you pass the Londonderry County Education Authority school, clearly marked: The Haslett School. And the County would hardly name one of its schools after a family without good reason. The Chief Clerk to the Coleraine Rural

District Council was, for long, a Haslett. One of the Royal Navy's supreme Submariners was Vice-Admiral A.R.Hezlet of Aghadowey, son of Major General Hezlet and author of the history of the "B Specials". My own direct family can boast of a strong Haslett connection in the Roe Valley, first at Drumneecy, then Ballyleighery and ultimately at Dernaflaw and Derryork. Here we had the epitome of the Ulster-Scot tradition, small farmers, tenant farmers, immensely frugal and hard-working, the strictest of Presbyterians. Two of them, Uncle Bob and Uncle Alec, went into the stone-mason business and won contracts, single-handed, for installing marble panelling at the Kelvin Hall in Glasgow and (in the eyes of every Belfastman) at that even more prestigious edifice, the ornate Belfast City Hall when it was being put up in the first few years of this century. And it was a delight one morning a year or two ago, to hear their direct descendant Malcolm Haslett of the B.B.C. World Service, reading and translating from the Russian newspapers with Brian Redhead in Moscow.

I was also struck by the Christian names favoured by the family of William Hazlitt, both before and after his time: William, John, William, John. The genealogist knows to place some weight on such a distinctive pattern of names. If the pattern had run: Jasper, Rupert, Jasper, Rupert I should have paid little attention; but the close similarity to the pattern of Christian names I knew so well in County Derry right down to the present day made me think.

Then there is the factual matter of his father's theological training. Hazlitt tells us in plain words that his father had been sent by his parents to the University of Glasgow to prepare for the Presbyterian ministry – a picture familiar in every Presbyterian home in Antrim and Derry whence the Scottish coast can be seen on a clear day. The local legends often have the added poignancy of a description of the tub of butter in the student's luggage to help pay for his lodgings. Altogether rather more an Ulster connection, one would think, than a Munster one.

There remains, you may argue, the stumbling block of the disparity in the spelling of the family name itself: Hazlett, Hezlet, Haslett and so on. Not so. I have learned to disregard small discrepancies in the recording of family names in the earlier centuries. Not until compulsory registration of births, deaths and marriages had been established during the nineteenth century, followed shortly by compulsory universal education, did the spelling of names become to any degree standardized. I have noted down countless discrepancies on headstones side by side recording, from the same townland and on the same grave, a Douglass and a Douglas, a Fleming and a Flemming, a Dunseith and a Dunceith, a Ray and a Wray. After having anguished in the early years of my work on family history over such differences, and after having puzzled over their possible significance, I learned to put the whole problem in perspective. I now openly dismiss it. I have proven the point far beyond any argument by recording, elsewhere, no fewer than twelve variants in the spelling of one of my family names: Morell, Morrell, Murial etc. and fully as many in the spelling of Shearer, Sherrard, Sherer, Shirer and so on. So: the little matter of an 's' or a 'z' in these findings of the Haslett clan are of no importance.

On looking up my own Notes recently I was further encouraged by finding one of our own Hasletts of Dernaflaw commemorated on a headstone as "Hazlett" with two daughters bearing the lovely names of Letitia and Hadessa.

All these observations and conclusions pointed me, independently, in the direction of a North Ulster origin for William Hazlitt.

Turning to the Dictionary of National Biography, that work of "stainless integrity" (if I may use Hazlitt's own phrase), I found the firm statement: "William Hazlitt, son of William grandson of John, originally of County Antrim". That re-inforced the pattern I was beginning to trace; and did so with great authority.

Then running through the various published "lives" of Hazlitt, I at last came upon the definitive story. It is by that most perceptive writer and student of Irish affairs, the Rt.Hon. Augustine Birrell.

Tradition tells us, he writes, of Hazlitts or Hasletts to be found in Antrim and in Coleraine and other parts of the North of Ireland. They were Protestants, "though affecting the Presbyterian colour" (an odd phrase to choose for such a stern attachment). One of them, a John Haslett, was a flax merchant – where better to deal in flax in the eighteenth century than in Antrim and Derry? – recorded around 1735. Eventually he grew rich and went off to set up business at Shrone Hill, County Tipperary. Some descendants of his still (Birrell was writing in 1902) live in the Tipperary region. Other Hasletts, needless to say, emigrated to America, notably a Col. John Haslett of the Coleraine branch of the family. Augustine Birrell's work bears all the hallmarks of careful, original research and gives much relevant detail. I feel justified in relying on Birrell as he was a Barrister, a Bencher, a Professor of Law and the author of several substantial works. Knowing something of the unhappy end to his career, as Chief Secretary in Ireland under the British Crown at the time of the 1916 Rebellion, we may reasonably wish – as he may well have wished himself – that he had stuck to biography and literature.

Although I have not found any Hasletts in the records of the main Plantation of Ulster under King James the First in the earliest years of the 1600s, I see them as part of the flood of Scottish Presbyterians who kept coming over to Ulster in successive waves during the seventeenth century and forming an integral, recognizable, recorded part of the Ulster-Scot tradition. I was pleased, the other day, to find among my own Notes a firmly authenticated reference to a Hazlitt attending First Dunboe Church (Castlerock) in 1663 along with – and this is significant – other undoubted immigrants from Southern Scotland: Fulton, Morrison, Oliver and so on. Little does it matter which combination of 's' or 'z', 'e', or 'i' a tired clergyman or his clerk may have thrown together on the church register, any wet, cold day after a baptism, a marriage or a funeral and by the poor light of a dim oil lamp.

In these matters I always do what I can to try to trace the Ulster-Scot settlers back to their undoubted origins in Scotland, a lonely, thankless task to which I have devoted my single-handed efforts for many years now. For William Haslett I can firmly cite: "John Heslett (an old spelling of Haslett or Hazlitt) waulker, burgess of Glasgow, 1575". Here I am quoting verbatim from the greatest authority on Scottish names, G.F.Black.

And similarly down to the present times. One of my best friends in life has been William Haslett of County Deny, my first cousin, an unusual man of many parts – farmer, teacher, philosopher, seeker after abstruse religions, and above all enviable collector of colleagues, neighbours, cronies, oddities, professors, visitors and unsuspecting hosts. Is it any wonder that I claim both William Haslett and William Haslett as my kinsmen? Let me repeat some lines I wrote in an obituary notice for one of these cousins in 1992:

A bunch of friends, college mates, professional colleagues, neighbours were the hall-mark of William Haslett's long, varied and surprising life. But the point is that they had a reality and an importance far beyond the scope of mere ceilidh and gossip. They sustained him loyally during his later years of acute pain and confinement. They made it possible for Leslie and him to go on living in what might seem, to the uninformed, the isolation of Whitehead, County Antrim. And as final proof of their affection and devotion they were all there to support Leslie and the family at one of the most impressive cremation funerals in modern Ulster, that Wednesday in January 1992.

All in all, and taking the genealogical liberties which any searcher in the field of family history in Ireland is entitled to allow himself, I take my stand on the belief that William Haslett, one of the greatest essayists in the English language, was indeed my distant cousin and an Ulsterman.

If any reader has enjoyed these present memoirs, then he or she is advised to consider some of the author's earlier published books:

Ulster Today and Tomorrow, PEP 1978
Girl, Name Forgotten. ... Littlewood Press 1991
Personalities at Poppelsdorf, Wm Sessions 1991
Aspects of Ulster, Greystone Press 1994
Working at Stormont, Institute of Public Administration, Dublin 1978